Exploring
the
Poetic Matrix
Musings on Us and the Planet
and How we are in the World

by

John (poet) Peterson

Special leather Dust Jacket, designed and
hand-tooled by Craig Peterson;
available upon request and with
an additional cost.

PM Library
An Imprint of Poetic Matrix Press
www.poeticmatrix.com

Dedicated to my Dear Friend

James Peak Downs

Geese river

I look up   surprised
to see three geese   bountiful
black long curving necks   ending in

white bonnets and black beaks   rocking
back and forth as they mutely
swim up river

they turn and stop at a bank
to turn up bugs   this trio
of hungry angels

one on the bank lifts
her neck on high
looking   white-bottomed birds of grace:

the irony of it   you want to see
geese in flight   but then they would be
gone   swimming one at a time in a line

wings folded back along sleek and sassy bodies
you sense they know of things
you will never see in your time   but

oh to witness world-curving necks!   they fly
in a ballet of white and black
and call out to each other "geese river"

The Beginning

In 1997 James Downs and I started Poetic Matrix Press, publishing primarily poetry. The name came from my involvement over many years in a number of areas. At the time we started the press I hadn't articulated these areas as they had been a part of my own journey through years of education and writing. James and I were working and living most of our time in Yosemite National Park. The opportunity to live and write in a place as beautiful as Yosemite surely was amazing. A few years earlier I had an opportunity to read my poetry at a Yosemite Centennial Celebration at the Awahnee Hotel of work written in and about Yosemite. I came to realize that spending time in the natural world and finding wilderness was fundamental to my poetry.

After gaining a Bachelor Degree in Philosophy and Art I began a serious long term study into consciousness, healing and meditation. Also, over many years, I had been writing and studying poetry and poets. Having been born in the era of Beat poetry and having been raised in the San Francisco Bay Area being influenced by Gary Snyder, Michael McClure, Lawrence Ferlingettii and yes, Allen Ginsburg and, very much by Lew Welch, was inevitable.

This work is a kind of bringing these resources together. A long period of time has passed since my exploration began. In the time that has elapsed, much of what I address here has gone on to become integrated into our cultural life. Among others, Bruce Lee introduced a new understanding of oriental ideas of truth and the relation of body, mind and spirit. Accupucture with Dr. Oh, Tai Chi at the Taoist Sanctuary, Gentle Yoga with Alma, meditation, mindfulness, and many more disciplines, have become important to so many of us.

Over the centuries, culture after culture have discovered/ rediscovered much of what I speck to here. In a recent article in *the Edge*, by Gregory Puente, a Nima (consecrated shaman) in the Bwiti tradition titled: *Jesus, Christ, God and You: What's the Difference?* says: "In the Bwiti tradition, Christ is known as Mbomba Eyano, among many other names. In other traditions it's called the Higher Self, Eternal Self, Krishna Consciousness, Buddha Consciousness, God Consciousness, Atma, Fire Snake, Winged Snake, etc. Although they have different names, all religions and spiritual paths talk about this consciousness, because all these paths lead to the same place."

And not just religions but all of us discover/rediscover what is inherently a fundamental part of what it means to be human. Sometimes we write it out, sometimes we sing it or dance it or paint it. Mostly we experience it in the many diverse ways we as humans of all races, genders, education, cultures, individuals and groups have of manifesting it and we pass it along to family and community and the larger social experience in our lives. Here I show some of what has been my experience.

Here are a couple of earlier pieces exploring some sources.

A Place In Which We Can Live
Reprinted from
The No-Street Poet's Voice
September 1987

While sitting in an apple orchard near Julian, in the Cuyamaca Mountains east of San Diego, celebrating the recent Harmonic Convergence (summer 1987) with some friends, I reflected on the significance of community and of the way voices sounding together open up the dream of each person involved. How movement and color together with imagination brings a vision from the shadows and how art is both a greater and a lesser vehicle for a people's desires.

Community comes about through artistic acts it seems. Jose Arguelles, poet, artist, and author, who focused the Harmonic Convergence in his book The Mayan Factor, states that it is art and the creative act that will bring in a new cycle. "Nothing else has worked thus far in solving the problems of militarism, environmental pollution, and social discontent, so why not give art, artists, and the creative spirit a try." [1] Community is generated by people creating and recreating their lives through greater and lesser artistic acts.

In their introduction to Pablo Neruda's Twenty Poems, James Wright and Robert Bly say, in reference to Neruda; "Once a poet takes a political stand, the wise assure us that he will cease writing good poetry [yet] at least half of his greatest work one must admit was written after [he became political]." Neruda wrote of his community's needs, dreams, and aspirations.

Garcia Lorca, the great Spanish poet, wrote that it is duende, "a power and not a construct...of blood...in sum, the earth-force, [that] is sustaining in art. The arrival of the Duende always presupposes a radical change in all forms as they existed on the old plane. It gives a sense of refreshment unknown until then, together with that quality of the just-opened rose, of the miraculous which comes and instills an almost religious transport."[2]

Each poem, each artistic act, if it lives, draws from the blood passion of the earth to bring life and the way we live into being and it stands or falls with the voice we bring to it. Where is there greater risk. And when is there a greater need for such artistic acts then now? Poetry is community because:

The poet's eye, in a fine frenzy rolling,
Doth glance from heaven to earth, from earth to heaven
And as imagination bodies forth
The form of things unknown, the poet's pen
Turns them to shapes and gives, to airy nothing
A local habitation and a name. [3]

And we and they will live inside of this.

There is a need for the poet's "diving into the wreak" to chart a path, to give voice to the shadows. There is a need for the poet to blend with the natural world and be a voice that speaks from the hidden world of nature into the visible culture. Here and now is a particularly critical time for poets to speak precisely and create community; creating a place in which we can all live. If not the poet then who fills the voice but the Oliver Norths amongst us?

Living as we do along geo-political, racial, gender, and economic borders gives us the need and the opportunity to speak "the form of things unknown;" and, if the daring is there, so too may be "that quality of the just-opened rose."

1. An interview with Jose Arguelles by Barbara Hand Clow.
2. "The Duende: Theory and Divertissement" by Federico Garcia Lorca in The Poet's Work, ed. Reginald Gibbons.
3. William Shakespeare, from A Midsummer Night's Dream.

Why do this?

First printed in Poetic Matrix Newsletter

This is the first of a continuing series of letters on the field of living that I call the Poetic Matrix. A true believer might claim that poetry was the essential stuff of life but that is true mostly of poets and some artists and affected lovers and others.

In an essay in San Diego's poetry monthly No Street Poet's Voice in the mid-eighties I wrote about poetry that creates "a place in which we can live" realizing that I had lived inside the life of some of the poetry that I later read. What is this kind of poetry that we can write intentionally and that can be "a place in which we can live?" This question is in part what this on-going letteR is about. (read that original essay - A Place In Which We Can Live - above.)

Poetry comes in many guises as does all art. Much poetry is therapeutic for both the reader and the writer; confessions of past karma; working out the confusions of life in the late age of america. Some has the power to change the world, for the good we hope, or at least to lay open the ills of the world. The poetry written around the Gulf War did more I suspect to expose to our soulfulness the error of that war than could even be imagined. This kind of poetry must continue. But still there is a kind of poetry that when read or heard or felt is just that, a feeling that is a strange awakening both to what is and to what is possible. For what is, we nod in recognition and breath into it. For what is possible, we sit and muse on it and hence, open a place in our being for it to grow. This is the poetry that is "a place in which we can live" and it is this that I am mostly interested with, but of course the other kind of poetry gets us on the road to this place and we will look at them as well from time to time.

> "...discover the poetic matrix
> which underlies poetry, art, and
> daily living. ...access new and
> magical entrances into the poetic
> experience."
> - from the Taoist Sanctuary of
> San Diego brochure on a class
> titled Meditation and the Poetic Matrix

sierra poem

i love it when
the sun shows
under clouds low
on the horizon
making scrawled patterns
on the foothills

violet mountains
lifted up behind

i see green
in that diffuse
light

i saw it that way once
behind my eyes

still the poem only
gets close

sometimes
i have to stop
and look
and feel my nerves excite
spreading across my body
letting in emerald
dark green earth
purple liquescent yellow
sun blowing light
across granite outcropping
into red grey
thunderheads

breath deep
and do not forget

if it's a good poem
find the thing it says
and have it

I hope some of this will be of interest in some small way. This is in no way a formal dissertation. It is a bringing together of essays, comments, poetry, studies, stories, reflections and even some exercises, intended to show both what came about and how. I leave it to the reader.—John

Contents

Exploring the Poetic Matrix

Dedicated to

James Peak Downs
Geese river

Exploring the Poetic Matrix

The Healing Body
Part I

Healing the Planet
Part II

Poetry, Poets, the Poem and the
Political Process Part III

A Discussion of Poetics: the Development of Wholistic Forms of Consciousness and Poetry Part IV

Meditation Part V

Appendix

Exploring
the
Poetic Matrix

Somewhere down there

Somewhere down there, through the moisture, the luminous haze
there is a single light, within the sphere of that light are others

like myself that I will never know. Their life, like mine, will blaze
from this to that, something of us may mingle in the moisture

that even now lies between us. From the earliest time I have looked
for a single place where no footprint has been, like in the middle

of all those red rocks. Back in the dark I have looked into windows
and cars, seen people I will not know. My life will not know

the same ache that even now pierces their heart.

-

The Healing Body
Part I

Perspective on the Planet

For many years radical thinkers and activists of many stripes have talked of the fragile and precarious state of the planet. They speak of the breakdown of ecosystems and the threat to the life of many species including our own. In recent years concerns about climate change, the rising temperature of the earth due to human activity, have become central. This has become an area not only of great concern but of great activity that has lead to much good and significant change on both the environmental and the political front. But still the problem is with us and it appears that it will be with us for some time.

Seeking the means to insure our future, R. Buckminister Fuller said, "I am a passenger on the spaceship Earth." It seems we must hold two compatible propositions with action issuing from them toward a resolution of an ancient conflict. The two propositions are: first, that the earth must be allowed to heal and return to her state of fullness while she is protected from future encroachment and misuse; and second, we as humans can live in harmony with the earth and, as we do, we will naturally find a healing that will make this a reality. This harmony will allow both the healing and the exotic and extraordinary avenues of culture to occur. The action that will issue from these two propositions, likewise, is natural and, more rightly, is the Taoist action of non-action, the allowing of the healing and creating of culture to take place and not the making of it.

What Is Wu Wei?[1]

One of Taoism's most important concepts is wu wei, which is sometimes translated as "non-doing" or "non-action." A better way to think of it, however, is as a paradoxical "action of non-action." Wu wei refers to the cultivation of a state of being in which our actions are quite effortlessly in alignment with the ebb and flow of the elemental cycles of the natural world. It is a kind of "going with the flow" that is characterized by great ease and awake-ness, in which—without trying—we're able to respond perfectly to whatever situation arises.

It is the removal of the structures that will not allow that which is natural to achieve that which is natural, an earth in its fullness and a people akin to it.

But the present world poses propositions far different from these and sets up conflicts that appear to make this reality impossible. And so, from time to time, it is important to seek the roots of the apparent conflict that has us set on a very destructive course. The "real world" of our present social life gives necessity to a social expansionist view; the necessity of a "growth economy" and the psychological imperative of domination as a primary underpinning of survival. So much of the current social milieu still operates under these major social viewpoints even after so many years of seeing the limitations these views force on the populace. Once one enters the primary social games, particularly business and politics, these imperatives become almost absolute so deeply are they held and so completely have they determined the way the social interactions are played out. It begins to appear that they themselves are part of the fabric of the nature of reality, though they lead to its ultimate demise; which is a contradiction so extraordinary that we blanch at its possibility. We have, it seems, habituated to a process that is destructive to ourselves and to the earth.

In the clear need to live in a harmonious relationship with the earth—healing both ourselves and the earth—while the prevailing "real world" continues its onslaught, a polarization is set up between earth and humanity; between conservation and economy; between that which is natural and the ever present need to explore new areas of culture. The desire to explore beyond the present known boundaries does not preclude the desire to maintain the intrinsic support of life, personally, socially, and as a planet. The need to experience the enchantment of social discovery and to experience the depth of feeling that the ancient earth can only give are not in opposition. Living inside the imperative of the planet's life does not preclude any of this.

These conflicts are not conflicts at all once we are able to free ourselves from the prevailing "real world" view but rather they are the play, the dance that propagates the endless change and variations that pass before us as life itself. As we enter the dance and exit the world of conflict we are privy to the harmony of the universe and recognize the boundaries where this too has a healing effect. And, when the boundaries have been breached in our personal, social, and planetary life, we lend ourselves to their rebuilding. Knowing when a healing need occur is a mark of maturity. And, as has been said in other places, now is the time for a mature response to the ills of the planet.

The Book

The Healing Body Part 1 of this work focuses on the healing of the person; *Healing the Planet Part 11* on our connection to the natural world where we can assist the earth's healing. It is important to point out here that a healing must occur simultaneously on the social level, particularly in the area of business; this healing may well be more traumatic. The propositions of the "real world" are being shown to be successful only in sustaining a small portion of the populace, failing in sustaining the vast population and failing to sustain the life of the planet. But, as the social reality is brought into harmony, the individual must continue their personal healing and the ecological healing must continue as well while the larger social healing moves forward.

Poetry, Poets, the Poem and the Political Process Part 111 deals with the political as it has such an impact on how we live. It has entered into my poetry over and over.

A Discussion of Poetics: the Development of Wholistic Forms of Consciousness and Poetry Part IV explores this same material by delving into the nature of poetry and poetics to not only look at the historical context for the revolutionary changes we are in the midst of but into the psychic context through the poetic line. Within the beauty realm of poetry and art we might find a creative space to grow our new conscious awareness. The process of poetry and a poetic gives insight into the nature of creating culture that is in harmony with the earth of our habitation.

7

Meditation Part V offers some practical exercises to place this discussion in the context of one's life.

It has been said that the only real problem for the philosophical mind is the exploration of god and, as this inquiry proceeds, at some point god must be the explicit topic as it is implicit in all of this. For the sake of this work I ask the reader to detach any reference to unity/love/ consciousness/god/spirit/soul from the socially expected religious interpretation; look toward a more global understanding.

*Rise leaving the indoor environment
Retire to the outdoors and breath
Move the body
stretching it into the surrounding world
of rocks and trees and moving air
Let music fill the intellect and revive it
Sit for a time and do nothing*

Some Metaphors

Many years back I spent some time researching and exploring in the area of a then emerging field called Biofeedback. Thanks to pioneers like Barbara Brown, Elmer and Alyce Greene, Joe Kamiya, and others, especially my good friend Lawrence Rouse, I gained important and extremely useful information and experience that allowed me to move into a very personal exploration of internal states of consciousness through physiological reality. The early research in biofeedback was an exploration of consciousness through the use of alpha brain waves as they related to states of consciousness described in mysticism east and west. Biofeedback as a healing form developed from this. In the intervening years this work has become a metaphor and a touch point for subsequent work.

At the same time I was introduced to the work of Oscar Ichazo and the Arica Institute. Here was advanced study into the nature of consciousness, unitary experience, and meta-concepts that made real in an experiential way the explorations that were underway. Many of the experiences of Arica form the foundation of my understanding and I give thanks to my friend Shakira Khan.

There have been times, through many years of travel, camping, poetry, and living in the mountains, where the natural world has been an unconscious place of rest and healing on the long journey toward untangling the web of the prevailing social reality. I now seek that connection consciously and I am grateful for that place of refuge and healing and ask only that my voice might be in service to the healing of the earth. Who can say who speaks for whom? The natural world has been a primary metaphor in my poetry as it has become the foundation for all that I do.

Biofeedback here is described as information and subsequent knowledge filtered through and drawn off the scientifically described systems of biology, anatomy, physiology, psychology, and neurology as they relate to an actual internal (or external) experience that a person has (or could have). I do not pretend to be an expert in any of these

9

fields, only an explorer for specific purposes. These experiences are then available as feedback, as a correcting mode, or feedforward, as a means of action. A more inclusive way of looking at biofeedback, getting closer to its core value, and one that incorporates feedback and feedforward as well as the entire environment of the body and the natural world, is body/mind/ecological-awareness (bmea). Biofeedback as a word symbol is limited in terms of what it denotes. It has built into it a sense of control due to the use of 'feedback', which in its primary use, is a correcting term.

Merriam-Webster Definition of feedback[2]

1 a: *the return to the input of a part of the output of a machine, system, or process (as for producing changes in an electronic circuit that improve performance or in an automatic control device that provide self-corrective action)*

2 a: *the partial reversion of the effects of a process to its source or to a preceding stage*

b: the transmission of evaluative or corrective information about an action, event, or process to the original or controlling source; also: the information so transmitted.

Wikibooks Negative vs Positive Feedback[3]

It turns out that negative feedback is almost always the most useful type of feedback. When we subtract the value of the output from the value of the input (our desired value), we get a value called the error signal. The error signal shows us how far off our output is from our desired input.

Positive feedback has the property that signals tend to reinforce themselves, and grow larger. In a positive feedback system, noise from the system is added back to the input, and that in turn produces more noise. As an example of a positive feedback system, consider an audio amplification system with a speaker and a microphone. Placing the microphone near the speaker creates a positive feedback loop, and the result is a sound that grows louder and louder. Because the majority of noise in an electrical system is high-frequency, the sound output of the system becomes high-pitched.

In order to advance beyond the control stage it is important to be able to utilize information in a positive feedback or feedforward manner and for taking in the entire body/mind/nature environment, and so the term must be expanded. Changing the positive signal, 'noise', into a usable value makes for a significant building of the signal.

Though, in my early biofeedback exploration, the use of electronic equipment was of great value, eventually they fell away to greater internal body awareness. As we approach a more inclusive state we can then prepare for the stage of letting information utilize us in its role as the ecological carrier for the natural world about us.

Information in this context is not the plethora of fact, data and accumulated extraneous bits and pieces that proliferates in the so-called information age. Information, it seems, is more the host of particulars that inform us that we are on the path of truth. We must have the ability to recognized these truths and sort them out from the mass of basically irrelevant data, i.e. deceit and mendacity, that surrounds us more and more in this odd age.

The ability to recognize information as truth may be the most important ability that an individual and a culture gains. Without it there is no intrinsic value to one's life or to the life of the community and eventually one wakes up to a pervasive meaninglessness. With it one is able to move with a sense of ease through the many convolutions of life sloughing off what is of little value. Separating what is transitory, faddish, or time bound from what is of lasting value no matter the language or cultural form it is wrapped in, is of fundamental importance to a highly functioning person and society.

How to recognize the truth in information is what we as a people are suppose to do in our family life and the education we give to our children. Yes, philosophers and clergy can think and reflect on the deep meaning here but it is our job as parents and educators to insure our young folk and, hence our adults, are prepare to discern these matters daily. That is at least in part what is writing is about. May it serve this end.

Nature, on the other hand, is a term almost too broad in its usage. It can contain everything if one desires to use it in the most trivial way. Here I will use it as referring to those experiences that provide us with our sense of earthly connectedness. Nature hosts those points of reference that give us a sense of the natural order of things and those experiences where we recognize that we are not the force behind the event, as in the movement through the seasons, but can, and also must, join with these forces to be fully animated with life. I use it in the sense of ecology, the interconnectedness of systems that play off of one another and operate in a complex balance with one another.

Body/mind/ecological-awareness assists us in integrating with this sense of nature and likewise can assist in the development of a subtle intelligence where the universal needs of human beings are satisfied and beyond which intelligence can take up the exciting task of designing configuration of mind in concert with nature; in the creating of culture. Nature likewise is not seen as being merely a support system for intelligence but is recognized as a vast living complex, intelligent and open to exploration, open to living in harmony with, in being part of, learning from, and much, much more. It is indeed the ground geologically and psychologically of our being as well as our ground spiritually.

Nature of the System

Starting in the 1970s the healing approach that this work presupposes was called Holistic (or Wholistic) Health. By some this movement in health is often called Integrative or Alternative Health or some other such term. Sometimes in the interest of appealing to a general population we fail to state what it is we are really about. To the extent we do this we do everyone a disservice; using Alternative rather than Holistic is such a disservice. Holistic has something to say about the process. And yet, as I have come to this work over many years, I want to give a wider reading and speak really of healing and health.

First

It is a bit strange but before getting into this first discussion I must place a disclaimer. After working with this material for many years, I find that there is an error of almost monumental proportions. Either I must handle this problem or abandon this work. This initial section lays a fundamental ground work for much of the rest of the work and so, if this premise is flawed, then much of the rest that comes may well be flawed as well. One of the benefits of working on this for many years is that I do indeed grow and learn and gain experience and so change can and, as it seems, must come as well. Here is one of those growth and change moments. I would like to quote the following, with which I agree in principle.

Holistic Health

by Suzan Walter, MBA co-founder of the American Holistic Health Association [4]

"Holistic Health is actually an approach to life. Rather than focusing on illness or specific parts of the body, this ancient approach to health considers the whole person and how he or she interacts with his or her environment. It emphasizes the connection of mind, body, and spirit. The goal is to achieve

maximum well-being, where everything is function-
ing the very best that is possible. With Holistic
Health people accept responsibility for their own
level of well-being, and everyday choices are used to
take charge of one's own health."

This has been essentially my operating definition for these many years since I became familiar with Holistic Health. But, and here is where my growth occurred, in my roll as publisher of Poetic Matrix Press I met and published a work by Leroy Moore, *The Black Kripple Delivers Poetry & Lyrics.* Leroy is a black, disabled man who has lived with his disability since birth and where removal of that disability is not an option. Recently I published another book of poetry, *Whispers of Krip Love Shouts of Krip Revolution,* by Lateef H. McLeod also a black disabled man. These two men taught me that some of the premises that I have been operating under needed a deep and fundamental change and so here I make those changes.

Sometimes we operate under assumptions that we did not even realize we had. Here I believe we carry the "perfect man" assumption. A false assumption that somewhere there is a perfect, idealized persona that not only are we a copy of but that we can aspire to and that is given to us by another idealized being, call it God, savior, hero, Superman, Jesus.

We, it seems, define holistic healing as being this idealized persona. Here and now I want to fundamentally and completely abandon that persona. It does not belong to us, anyone of us ever. We are in truth each one a configuration of US. We are indeed, who WE are, not the emanation or imagination of some super being, whether Jesus or Thor! And so we must alter one of the first premises of holistic healing. I state it here as I wrote it so many years ago with changes.

The first premise on which a Holistic healing process
depends is that a personal experience of wholeness
for US must be available. An experience of oneself as
a complete person physically, emotionally, mentally,
spiritually, and ecologically needs to be available
in the healing process. This must be an experience

and not a theory or concept to be expounded. Various theories and concepts, various procedures and techniques may be utilized in order to aid one in attaining this experience and various devices may be used to describe it once attained but the having of it is central. Therefore, fundamental to any procedure that could be called Wholistic is that it allows for and encourages a glimpse of what it is like to feel whole as it relates to each individual. A person who is ill or lost in the "real world" must be able to get, in the course of the healing experience, a momentary experience that can give one a sense of their value and worth, without debilitating pain. This experience must also go beyond to a glimpse of what for them is true well-being.

I extend it now to make an accounting.

The first premise of healing is that a personal experience of wholeness must account for the variance of self both real and, as it were, idealized. What it must not be is some extra idealized entity outside of the real person and the real personal experience. It seems in our rather strange journey as a specie we have found it necessary to find some super-being in our various god myths that we are, must be, and must proceed to be. The Marvel Universe is a recent example of how we have come to re-energize the Nordic myths as the Abrahamic and Hinduic myths have come to dominate our current world view. To the extent that these characters have value, then they have benefit. To the extent that they have but power, they are of no value to us.

I will continue my discussion and will introject again at various point.

During our first encounter with the wholistic movement in the mid 70s a Chinese gentleman, James Wang, came through Fresno. James came in the tradition of the barefoot healers in China. James would come to town and stay with one member of the community or another. He would join some at dinner and would set up evenings where he would talk with us about Chinese medicine and healing and give Acupuncture treatments to those of us who were fascinated with this very different healing form. As we lay back on the table and he placed needles in specific points described by Chinese Medicine for over 3000 years, soft music would relax us. During the process of re-balancing our interior life utilizing the needles and these points, we would drift off gaining that first experience that we were looking for, a sense that there indeed was a place of wholeness that we might find in the tragedy of the day. James came through town a number of times and then no more, he may well still be out there finding those who need this moment of wholeness to encourage them on their way.

Also, central to holistic healing is the acceptance of a human-istic approach for all parties. Recognizing the healing process in terms of a living person involved in the experiences and problems, joys and follies of living, rather than seeing a disease or dysfunction, is key. What is to be healed is a person not an illness. There are cultures where it is not acceptable to say for instance "you have cancer." To say such a thing is itself invasive and may enhance ill health rather than assist healing.

> Linda Ann S.H. Tom, M.D. discusses these sorts of cultural difference in Health and Health Care for CHINESE-AMERICAN ELDERS[5]
> 1. Karma. Bad luck to talk about illness or death, as it may cause it to happen (McLaughlin & Braun, 1998).
> 2. Advance Directives/End of Life Issues: Many Chinese may be reluctant to discuss these issues due to the belief that if you talk about something bad, it could occur (karma).

The resolution of the health problem—physical, mental, emotional, or spiritual—may entail changes in life style, attitude, and relationships as well as the obvious medical treatment. Here there is an approach to healing that sees an illness as seeking balance in the person's life. This is different from the Western medical approach that, in its extreme, looks at an illness as a mechanical problem and treats the illness as such. Yet we know that in the Western medical approach it is not possible to leave this humanistic approach behind.

> *A heart procedure at St. Agnes Hospital in Fresno showed how fundamental to the healing process this wholistic approach truly is. The setting, the hospital staff, the doctors, family, spiritual communities, friends, familiar and as yet unmet, and the healing energies of god all come to play a part in the healing process.*

Wholistic healing assumes that the cure of the illness is contained in the illness and in fact the illness is a message to the person that something is not right in their life. That is not to say that illness is karma. Or, as we have noted, that all that constitutes us is an illness at all. Life is a vast complex where accident, serendipity, and circumstance all play their part in that which is US. Holistic health is a learning process as well as a healing process. In a wholistic healing process the individual has the responsibility for their own wellness and the professional is a resource person helping to steer them in directions that may prove fruitful.

Another primary premise is the concept of the whole being greater than the sum of its parts so that focusing on the whole greatly enhances the scope of the organism's healing. Of importance here is a shift in the figure/ground or parts/whole relationships. Once one leaves the University it is very rare that a discussion of the nature of life and reality occurs but this discussion may well be critically important to the understanding of the source of a health issue. In the traditional Western medical approach the focus on the parts tends to supersede an interest in the whole. In a holistic approach the ground is brought forward and recognized as the source point not only of the problem but ultimately the source point of the healing of the problem. Shifting to a ground/figure, whole/parts perspective while maintaining awareness of them both allows the conceptual shift to the whole being greater than the sum of its parts. By focusing on the whole one creates a greater, more functional being to which the parts relate in a more integrated, coordinated, and aesthetic way. In terms of healing, by focusing on the whole a natural healing occurs in the parts.

The Over-soul—Ralph Waldo Emerson [6]

We live in succession, in division, in parts, in particles. Meantime within man is the soul of the whole; the wise silence; the universal beauty, to which every part and particle is equally related, the eternal ONE. And this deep power in which we exist and whose beatitude is all accessible to us, is not only self-sufficing and perfect in every hour, but the act of seeing and the thing seen, the seer and the spectacle, the subject and the object, are one. We see the world piece by piece, as the sun, the moon, the animal, the tree; but the whole, of which these are shining parts, is the soul.

Biofeedback, from which body/mind/ecological-awareness derives, emerged from a period of growth that had as one of its central purposes the experience of a wholistic condition. Although the discovery of biofeedback occurred simultaneously, and often serendipitously, in many places—in the work of Joe Kamiya, Barbara Brown and others—the context (the ground) from which it emerged was personal growth, the use of LSD and other mind-altering chemicals; the rediscovery of Eastern spiritual systems and the development of new Western psychologies. Consciously at times and unconsciously at others there was the desire for a unifying, more encompassing experience that would break people out of a society enmeshed in a fragmented, disintegrated preoccupation with parts that were either not working or that were destroying vast arenas of the social, personal, and environmental fabric; racism, the Vietnam War, pollution are just some of many examples of the societal problems that were paramount during the formative year of the 1960s and 70s.

Prior to these developments in our modern era it was very difficult to grasp the whole because the methods available in the prevailing social climate, the tools, techniques, philosophies, religions, etc., precluded this in their very form.

Biofeedback, in articles by Joe Kamiya and others all reprinted in Charles Tart's book *Altered States of Consciousness*, [7] plus Elmer and Alyce Green's work with Swami Rama, developed a tool and a framework to study and to experience new states of consciousness. The promise of yoga and Zen, as well as other Eastern spiritual methods, was that it was possible to obtain a direct experience of the whole; what biofeedback gave the West was a palatable tool to explore this possibility. The shift to a ground/figure relationship could be personally explored. What this exploration showed was that changing this focus brought about a very high, very integrated feeling state that was conducive to subjective descriptions of well-being, and showed optimal healing of the organism.

The non-specific focus on the whole has specific effects in healing. This is what was shown by the Greens' work on meditation, Transcendental Meditation, yoga, Benson's Relaxation Response, etc. By using a very non-specific device, a mantra for instance, very specific effects were found to occur in many physiological systems, healing occurred. This is what was inherent in the use of alpha and specific alpha frequencies. What we achieve in an alpha-centered state is a non-specific condition of wholeness; a holistic state that has significant beneficial effects for the overall organism. [8]

With a lab set up in a corner of the Chemistry Department by Lawrence, he and I, and a few others were able to practice our ability to utilize biofeedback (brainwave feedback) to alter various colored lights and musical notes. Sitting quietly in a darken room—with the use of LSD on occasions—we were able to make subtle changes in brain frequency and hence change the musical tone and the light color. A change on the interior affected a change on the exterior. Fancy that!

Another important realization that must come early in body/mind/ecological-awareness in order to be able to gain any facility with one's own interior is a realization that one ultimately comes to in working with nature. It is that one may come with intentionality to the particular task, one may want very much for a particular event to occur but, before it can occur, one must 'let go' and allow it to occur. One must get out of the way finally and let it happen.

If one's intentions correspond to the nature of the thing then, in all likelihood, it will occur, given that the organism (or nature) is not in a condition where it would be impossible for it to achieve that state. What is import in all of this discussion is that we are in a discovery mode, for ourselves, and so we must, at each juncture, determine what WE are. What is the criteria that describes the 'nature of the thing', that which provides the sound basis of our intentionality. As the self-discovery proceeds we are the determiner of who/what WE are.

Corresponding to the nature of the thing (US) has significance. When a person who is working at gaining voluntary control over one state or another persists at attempting willful control, then one may well get a confounding effect; a dichotomous condition is set up that necessitates the creation of an opposite. This seems to be a condition of the will when it is being exercised in a faulty manner, when it attempts to control rather than allow what is already there to be manifested. In a practical sense this means that an organism has the means to maintain its systems in what is for this organism the natural condition, if we will but release willful control. Nature as well will balance when left to her own devices.

Wisdom of the Body

Early popular accounts of biofeedback talked for the most part about gaining control over physiological systems through the information loop. It was possible to get very precise information about a variety of physiological systems, from muscle activity to cardiovascular function, skin temperature, and brain wave activity and to present this information in a usable way back to the individual through electronic devices. It was possible for a person to intentionally influence the operation of these systems and hence gain a measure of control over them. This proved startling in some cases because it had been thought impossible to gain this kind of voluntary control, as in the case of the autonomic nervous system. Many stress related illnesses were found to be amenable to this kind of intervention; for instance hypertension and tension headaches, TMJ.[9]

And yet a study of basic physiology refers to the variety of homeostatic mechanisms that are built into the human organism— from the built in need for rest to aid the entire organism, to specific mechanisms like the core body temperature homeostat.

Homeostasis is the property of a system within the body of a living organism in which a variable, such as the concentration of a substance in solution, is actively regulated to remain very nearly constant.

"Mammals regulate their core temperatures, using hypothalamic temperature sensors in their brains, but also elsewhere in their bodies. When core body temperature falls behavioral changes are set in motion which, in humans, include the donning of warmer clothes, the seeking out of wind-free, warmer environments, and, eventually, the curling up in the "fetal position" to reduce the surface area (skin) exposed to the cold.

"When body temperature rises, or skin heat sensors detect a threatening rise in body temperature, behavioral changes cause the animal to seek shade,

and, in humans, the sweat glands in the skin are stimulated via cholinergic sympathetic nerves to secrete a dilute watery fluid called sweat onto the skin, which, when it evaporates, cools the skin and the blood flowing through it. Panting is an alternative effector in many vertebrates, which cools the body also by the evaporation of water, but this time from the mucous membranes of the throat and mouth." [10]

That we have instruments and techniques to consciously monitor and alter these internal events has aided us in letting the 'wisdom of the body' reassert itself, finding those balance points that allow for health and healing to occur. So the original fascination with controlling internal states gives way to the fascination of finding those organic, natural states that allow the body to operate at its most natural level. Where this culminates in the recognition of a healthy internal state by giving us the feeling tone of well-being that is endemic to us, this is indeed the "wisdom of the body" that our body, in whatever state it is in, is previe to. It is not physiological gymnastics that are important, nor even health that is the final objective, rather health is the starting point towards realizations in significant areas of one's life.

In the beginning one needs to learn how to allow the internal environment to gain its determined healthy state. The primary assumption here is that the body, in its very form, has the capacity to do this without conscious intervention. The first step is to remove the accumulation of negative experience and, to the extent possible, remove the organic and biochemical blocks and deficiencies that stand in the way of achieving a "natural" state in the body/mind. "Natural" to the extent that this is a state available, in its particular manifestation, to each person no matter their other talents and capacities; where healing occurs; where health is, here all are equal.

One primary message that the body gives us, and which we so often fail to heed, whether it is because of circumstances in our external lives or past trauma, is relaxation. In our fast-paced, demanding lives, relaxation can do as much as anything to help remove negative experience, restore balance, and enhance healing in our lives. I am reminded of an interview with Sophia Loren, surely the most beautiful woman of our era. When asked if she had had plastic surgery, she said no and she never would. Then, when asked what her secret to maintaining her beauty was, she said, only two things, eat right and get lots of rest. Her secrets surely work. Rest and relaxation allows us to slough off the accumulated tensions of the day and restore the natural vibrancy of our body.

(See Relaxation Exercise in Appendix 1)

Necessity of Strong Support

Body/mind/ecological-awareness is information gathering that is then presented in a sequence of ways. At first, one is presented with random pieces that are very difficult to comprehend since in the beginning the maps of ones personal internal states are not well known. Second, one is presented with negative information or information that tells one in which direction you do not want to go. In our normal experience we know negative feedback as pain and/or punishment and so it is not very useful here. An understanding of negative feedback will need to be incorporated and will be described below. Third, bmea presents one with positive information that directs one towards a viable goal, the most basic of which is healing and individual norms. Fourth, one is presented with information as a matrix of states and conditions in the natural world, available to explore creatively.

In the first instance we have information generated that is confusing in nature. In order for this information to be usable two criteria must be met. First, the information must be significant and not merely noise. It must in fact be viable and represent the true condition to be measured and acted upon. The information gathering device or method must be viewing or experiencing the proper signal, and presenting or representing this signal in a way that is in fact usable; it must have been determined at some point what the usable signal was and what it represented. The exercise in relaxation gives us the first set of clues about our body's held tensions.

The source of the signal must be of a nature to allow one to build off of it toward a viable state. I refer here to the biological source of the signal and the necessity for that biological source to be of a kind to allow maximal utilization of the signal toward individual function. There is a difficulty here in using a source that is not recognized as the primary norm for the individual. Establishing that norm must preceed first or it may not be possible to move to a fully functional use of the signal. But we are here addressing the use of bmea as a means of moving toward healing and a healthy state so doubts about the value of the material we are working with must be handled early on. This is a primary question that must be in place.

This question is a major source of the next move to negative feedback, in the best use of negative feedback. We need to have confidence and continually utilize the negative feedback. We need to constantly evaluate the signal and what it reflects. This question will in the long run keep us on a course that guides us toward the condition where the question will no longer have meaning; we will then be inside the ecological awareness of the body/mind and nature where a fuller awareness will be in operation.

The next move in negative feedback is where the information received tells us about the condition we are in. The body, in many respects, operates on negative feedback. When you are in a deficient mode you receive a negative signal to correct. A nociceptor ("pain receptor") is a sensory neuron that responds to damaging or potentially damaging stimuli by sending "possible threat" signals to the spinal cord and the brain. If the brain perceives the threat as credible, it creates the sensation of pain to direct attention to the body part, so the threat can hopefully be mitigated; this process is called nociception.[11] Pain is not the object but is a signal of something that is actually going on.

By beginning to read the negative signal we begin to open to the 'wisdom of the body'; we begin to recognize the signals that tell us a particular condition is causing a problem, minor at present, major later on. We begin to read the messages of the body. And so negative feedback is always a correcting signal, changing direction toward either a predetermined norm, or changing direction seeking a more functional state, guiding us to momentary states of well-being that are the first clue to a healing condition.

Positive feedback in the body comes into play when a system has begun to move in the direction of greater functionality, greater integration, the predetermined norm, or when a more optimal state has been located. Positive feedback comes into play when we gain glimpses of a state of well-being and wish to enhance it; when we experience bliss, ecstasy, or the peace and calm of a high mountain meadow and recognize these pleasing states as desirable, wishing to incorporate these experiences into our everyday life.

The fourth move brings us fully into body/mind/ecological-awareness, where we recognize the information as a matrix of internal and external states, interconnected and fully functional no matter the consequence. At this point we will be required to recognize all conditions—healthy, enlightened, as well as difficult, in a new and altogether revolutionary way where each condition has value. We will then see the extraordinary possibilities of this new state of body/mind/ecological-awareness where information is a voice from the natural world of our body/mind and of the environment. The creative possibilities are endless and also lead us into creating in concert with the best and truest facts of nature.

> Antoni Gaudí, (1852-1926) the Spanish Catalan
> Modernist architect embodies this principle.
> "Under the influence of neo-Gothic art and
> Oriental techniques, Gaudí became part of the
> Modernista movement which was reaching its
> peak in the late 19th and early 20th centuries.
> His work transcended mainstream Modernisme,
> culminating in an organic style inspired by
> natural forms." [12]

We then go inside the ecological aspect of body/mind/ecological-awareness where we see the interconnectedness of our internal and external states and utilize the information presented as a recognition of our larger truer inner/outer nature. We begin to see the mostly arbitrary nature of our experience, the way our conditioning not only clouds our perception of events out there but interior events as well and how through a careless reading we attach greater and lesser value on these events, perceptions, experiences, concepts and the information that signals their arrival. Eventually we are lead quite naturally into a realization that all of these 'states' are merely the infinite conditioned variations of the universe both inner and outer and, as the Buddha taught in the Diamond Sutra, all conditioned existence is illusion:

> All composed things are like a dream,
> a phantom, a drop of dew, a flash of lightning.
> That is how to meditate on them,
> that is how to observe them. [13]

26

Outside the double doors a family of Dogwood
Stand   in the coming fall season
Inside and outside the air is the same
Still   in the afternoon with the sun gone
Behind Glacier Point
Dogwood family begins the first stage of
Change toward winter
A few leaves barely curling brown
Pulling ever so slowly
From the outward expanse of summer
To a deep place in the interior of their world

Blocking the Flow of Life

The beginning point in the process of returning to a harmonious relationship with the natural world, and hence with oneself, is to recognize the varieties of information that are coming off our body and our mind and to sort through the noise and confusion towards an understanding of what brought on the present condition. Since the time of Freud we have had a series of extremely good maps of the source of our negative conditioning. We know that the etiology of our present negative behavior has roots in our early experience, in our social conditioning, in the effect on our physiology brought on by our complex early experience. Many systems have been developed since Freud to work through the trauma of these early experiences.

This is not the place to dwell on any one of these systems; rather it is important to recognize the source of the present condition of one's life, particularly the source of one's negative experience. We begin the process of releasing the effects of negative experience when we recognize their source. The experiences do not go away, they are our experiences, but the effect on us is mitigated by our awareness of them.

> We are dominated by negative experience because over time they have built up a center where a free flow of energy is inhibited. This is where there is a build up of stress, toxins, karma, ego mechanism, inhibitions. The break-up of this negative complex requires the removal of the conditions that block the flow. This needs to be done at the particular point in the body where the build up occurs as well as in the mind-set that goes along with it.[14]

Working through the blockage must be done quickly and in a surgical way, too long and too extensive a look at the source of the blockage can lead in the long run to a preoccupation with these very mechanisms and, unless one is a professional, constant involvement can become thoroughly debilitating in its own right.

If a person is without a deep neurotic or pathological condition the break up of harmful mechanisms can be done with minimal difficulty. If the timing is right, the harmful domination of one's negative behavior can begin to lessen. If the breakup is not amenable in this way, then more extensive help must be garnered from professionals in the appropriate disciplines.

Both the negative and the positive aspects of one's personality develop from this energetic point of view because energy is held in an individual based on many criteria, ultimately too complex to be analyzed though not too complex to be known. A combination of physical characteristics, psychological structures, held beliefs, motivational principles, as well as the more esoteric aspects of talent and spiritual sources help create the complex of personality. The vast impact of family up-bringing, social conditioning, nutritional intake, the educational process that a person undergoes, and one's day-to-day interpersonal relationships all add to the growing person. The extent of one's opportunities, karma of birth, place in history, and the energy potential in the natural place of one's birth and up-bringing, as well as the conditions of the heavens, all of these and more influence one's nature and the formation of the personality that one moves through the world with. To the extent that the aggregate is healthy the formation will be healthy, but where trauma occurs, where conditions exist that are problematic, the effect can be negative. The term "post-traumatic stress disorder" came into use in the 1970s in large part due to the diagnoses of US military veterans of the Vietnam War. Here one needs to take a look at the experiences and come to some resolution about their influence.

Some years back I met a very personable man. Good looking, athletic, he was on the path of spiritual development. We met in a spiritual training; he had spent some years searching through a variety of spiritual disciplines.

One day during an outing at a park he told me of his early experiences. He had been raised in Brooklyn. As a child he very easily gravitated toward the *streets and the gang culture that predominated there for young boys his age.*

It was very much the West Side Story tale of the Sharks and the Jets for him. Rumbles were the normal activity for protecting turf and settling scores. But soon a change occurred. Soon the rumbles, the fights, the violence were not about settling scores or protecting turf, he began to truly enjoy the violence itself; he began to enjoy beating up on someone, inflicting pain. He participated in sports, particularly Hockey, with this same joy of inflicting pain. But again a change occurred. Soon it was not even about inflecting pain on others, it was about receiving the pain, getting beat up. He would go out with the express purpose of getting beat up, of getting pulverized into a bloody mass.

At this point some part of him woke up and he, unlike many others in his community, began the process of recognizing his condition and embarking on a path toward a spiritual recovery. Through all of his awakening though, he did not deny his past, he accepted it as a part of who he was but he put it in a perspective where it could do him and others no harm.

When I last saw him he was working in a Winery somewhere in Sonoma.

Enough parts broke down that something new could occur and change could take place. The path could be seen though it was vague and shadowy. And yet acceptance of the past could allow the future to be different rather than creating through denial another negative that would bring the old behavior out again in another form.

During a program of spiritual training, which was a very gentle form of meditation, movement, and touch, we invited a man who had a very different background from the participants to do a presentation. This man grew up in the very tough farm worker communities of the San Joaquin Valley. As a young man he would go to the bars that catered to the farm workers and, as was common, get into fights with the locals. Drinking and fighting were the way to blow off the difficult working and living conditions of the people in this poor community. Eventually he would even go into the surrounding cowboy bars where him being a Mexican insured that he would mostly come out on the poor end of the brawls.

Finally, beaten into a numbness by the conditions of living, work, and constant fights, he settled into a spiritual malaise. A friend invited him to a Karate class and he began to study this ultimate form of fighting with the clear goal of being able to beat up anyone in the cowboy bars. Finally, he felt he was ready and so he went back to the bars. But, rather than fight, he realized first, that he could do serious harm to another in a fight, and more importantly some of the spiritual discipline had begun to work on him and fighting lost its luster.

He continued his training. It was very rough because he was a very rough person. Baseball bats were used on shins and forearms to toughen them and the workouts were grueling but, through it all, his teacher began to instill the deeper principles of Karate and he began to understand his spiritual nature. By the time he spoke to us, Karate was a discipline to bring the mind into an awareness of the body and hence into harmony. He never denied his violent nature but he had found a receptive mode to allow the negative experiences of his life to flow into so that he could truly change himself and move along his spiritual path.

to movement

reach your hand into still air
and pull it
dig your fingers into damp ground
and bring it with you
spread your arms across the ridge
and make it rolling
place you hands at the oak tree's root
and raise it with you
send you chi upon the grass
and feel it bending
give your red eye to the hawk's wing
and learn its calling
make your heart the same with the land
and you'll be green

in mountains

lost in mountains
      extracted from books

i'll meet you on the trail
hidden by the bracken fern
and we shall breath

The Field
The Old Field

Reviewing one's present circumstances, up-bringing, religious background, social history, schooling, family, health, work life, community relations, philosophical underpinnings, etc. reveals one's present field of behavior; going deeper to the basic assumptions of the life of the community gives up the paradigm that animates unrecollected motivations. One operates inside the field and the paradigm. We have heard much of the paradigm shift that we are in the midst of. Thomas Kuhn, in his *The Structure of Scientific Revolutions* (1962), is credited with the initial description of the idea of paradigm shifts especially related to science. In *The Structure of Scientific Revolutions, p.12*[15] Kuhn wrote, "Successive transition from one paradigm to another via revolution is the usual developmental pattern of mature science."

Though not as absolute in the social sciences still paradigm shifts are critical. Marilyn Ferguson called attention to this shift some years ago in her book *Aquarian Conspiracy (1980)*.[16] She claimed that a shift from a patriarchal, authoritarian, domination of nature paradigm to a more balanced, cooperative, living within the reality of nature paradigm was occurring. I am not sure that we in this present age can ever make a complete shift into this new paradigm as we are dependent in our formative period on the old paradigm, still we do have a choice to make the shift if we are aware of where we are and where we are going. And we can see in various segments of society the paradigm shift beginning.

There is usually more than one field in which we must navigate at any one time. A paradigm is more encompassing than a field though they subsume one another. Here I am more concerned with the field in which one operates on a day-to-day basis. The field provides the stimuli and the cues for behavior. It determines choices and avenues of change. The field influences the subconscious dream (paradigm) which percolates into the conscious life and motivates behavior. It is persuasive but not totally consuming. A paradigm has a more consuming nature and it can be very difficult both to comprehend and to change without a great calamity that radically alters and undermines the prevailing paradigm.

With a shifting field we have the possibility of moving with some intention if we are aware of what is going on. A maturing outlook allows us to recognize that various people and communities operate in different fields of reality. How do we move within fields?

Dependence/Independence

Elmer and Alyce Green in their book *Beyond Biofeedback* speak of field independent and field dependent behavior.[17] They make a case for field independent behavior as it allows one to step back from their present circumstances and in an independent manner evaluate and make changes, particularly changes that lead to healing. Generally, the Greens say that a field independent status is more functional than a field dependent mode. Yet that position becomes limiting when seen in the extreme that it has been taken on both the environmental and biological level. It may well be that the old paradigm of domination creates a field independent position of an extreme sort. Nature is the biblical realm given to man and subsequently exploited. The body is seen as something to be controlled by the mind—mind over matter—creating the mind/body split that has accounted for so much destruction in nature and in one's health.

A field dependent mode has limitation in that we are deluded into believing that we are the disease, that we are incapable of truly affecting change and healing in our lives or affecting our environment in an effective manner. Yet there is great power in settling into the healing grace of nature or the security of a community of people and accepting that we are them. A field dependent position has the possibility for a great richness of experience and a truly transcendent perspective but it is faulted as being overly immersing and not allowing an individual to stand in one place and withstand the continuous onslaught of environment and biology.

A greater position than either is to have both, movement between a dependent and an independent relationship to the environmental field and the biological field.

Method

Knowledge about something is the equivalent of making space available to contain that thing. That is why knowledge allows one to absorb more of that thing and hence hold more energy or power. It is literally creating space where once there was held belief or fear or simply unused portions of the brain and body.

Every set of ideas or set of values is a configuration of energy in the body/mind and acts as a mechanism of creative potential, defenses (in the best sense), emotional protection, or vehicles for movement. The mind has been likened to a reducing valve by Aldous Huxley in *The Doors of Perception*.[18]

> "Reflecting on my [mescalin] experience, I find myself agreeing with the eminent Cambridge philosopher, Dr. C. D. Broad, "that we should do well to consider much more seriously than we have hitherto been inclined to do the type of theory which Bergson put forward in connection with memory and sense perception. The suggestion is that the function of the brain and nervous system and sense organs is in the main eliminative and not productive. Each person is at each moment capable of remembering all that has ever happened to him and of perceiving everything that is happening everywhere in the universe. The function of the brain and nervous system is to protect us from being overwhelmed and confused by this mass of largely useless and irrelevant knowledge, by shutting out most of what we should otherwise perceive or remember at any moment, and leaving only that very small and special selection which is likely to be practically useful." According to such a theory,

each one of us is potentially Mind at Large. But in so far as we are animals, our business is at all costs to survive. To make biological survival possible, Mind at Large has to be funneled through the reducing valve of the brain and nervous system. What comes out at the other end is a measly trickle of the kind of consciousness which will help us to stay alive on the surface of this particular planet."

To a large extent the knowledge base, set of ideas, and values are the gates of this valve. They act to filter out non-essential material and to allow in material that is pertinent to the person or community. This particular set gives the person or community a means to organize and channel the energy it is receiving. If the set is removed or breached the person can have a very significant experience of a positive nature that also can lead to difficulties in reorganization because one is flooded with input that prior to the breach was not observed or received. Psychedelic experiences are so enlivening because they open the valves, yet they can be problematic if one does not have a new field (or a new paradigm) in which to reorganize around.

What is needed is a larger, more complete framework in which to fit the new information, either a model that can account for the new sensations or a developed spiritual understanding that leads one to accept one's intuitive awareness. Likewise one may need a new and more creative method for channeling and out-putting the energy that has been received. During the early use of psychotropics, as they took users outside of the dichotomous realms of good/bad, heaven/ hell, God/Devil; Taoism and Buddhism provided a new context for understanding. Music and art provided a new creative outlet. Without these forms many users got into serious trouble.

Communication is also of importance in this new move. We contact one another through a language and that contact, that language or the reality that is created in the speaking and listening, opens the place for the new field to be recognized and for the new paradigm to be transmitted.

Garth Kemerling in Philosophy Pages (philosophypages.com) speaks about Ludwig Wittenstein regarding language: [19]

"Like the rules of a game, Wittgenstein argued, these rules for the use of ordinary language are neither right nor wrong, neither true nor false: they are merely useful for the particular applications in which we apply them. The members of any community—cost accountants, college students, or rap musicians, for example—develop ways of speaking that serve their needs as a group, and these constitute the language-game ... they employ. Human beings at large constitute a greater community within which similar, though more widely-shared, language-games get played. Although there is little to be said in general about language as a whole, therefore, it may often be fruitful to consider in detail the ways in which particular portions of the language are used."

"Even the fundamental truths of arithmetic, Wittgenstein now supposed, are nothing more than relatively stable ways of playing a particular language-game. This account rejects both logicist and intuitionist views of mathematics in favor of a normative conception of its use. 2 + 3 = 5 is nothing other than a way we have collectively decided to speak and write, a handy, shared language-game. The point once more is merely to clarify the way we use ordinary language about numbers."

One person contacts another person in a number of ways. One is to link with the particular energy arrangement of the person we are speaking with i.e. architects speak in architects language; truck drivers in truck drivers language; artists speak in their work in a language of color, shape, music etc., the viewer or listener learns the language of the art. Another method is to let go of one's own mental protective barriers and go directly into the pattern formation of the other person and speak what exactly is going on inside their matrix. Here one loses one's own identity for a time and gives energy to the

38

pattern of the other. This can be chancy as one can lose ones own energy and patterns in the process but if done with strength it can be very useful and instructive.

If we are willing to be explorers in the realm of knowledge and communication, new fields of behavior and new paradigms are open to us. Here we may gain access to the potentials of nature. Body, mind, eco-awareness, where we recognize the inner and outer as the source of our consciousness, allows us to move in a dependent and an independent manner, creating in concert with the natural world that is the source of our being.

Yosemite - Beneath Glacier Point

It's early, about 5:15 am, as I listen and extend across space; consciousness recognizes other consciousness and I am involved in the communication of speaker and hearer. The many birds in the Dogwood, Black Oak and Vanilla Puzzle Pine are speaking away. I am an eavesdropper but still there in our communion. Busy folks they are so early in the morning.

I wonder if in the maze of sound some kind of spiritual consistency emerges and they recognize themselves in their birdness, in their communion with love in their image.

Later the same day I walk out onto my porch and I hear the wind moving through the Dogwood leaves and I am struck why poets write of wind so often. It is a sound that perfectly resonates with the most fundamental nature of being. It is a sound out there that is coursing through the most inner intimate reaches of mind and body. The sound of wind touches nerve endings perfectly and we are immediately aware of how we are made, what our subtle self is made of. We and wind have made a recognition of each other and know who we are and who the world is. We have realized what the language of the soul is and in that recognition have found ourselves once again.

Later I step out and the sound of Stair Step Falls brings the recognition again. Sound, white noise that within carries all sound. They combine together into the same primordial sound that is us. OM is the sound of water, wind, bird, us in meditation as it contains all sound. Love is manifest and we are aware of love out there and in here and they are the same.

Here in this place with all the people as well, birds, wind, water, I and love have sounded.

wilderness

there is a constant journey
to nature   to wilderness

an awakening from history
 to the irrelevance of time

a movement from times back and forth
 the play of good and evil
 the decision to be this character or that
to the play of grass on the mesa
after a fall rain   each
   drop   balanced
on
    many   blades

the grass is green
the lush tone of the   green
  note   ringing

the door to the hillside drips
         in bronze   rust and amber
     yellow slips of light

small creatures line the edges
their robes flow through a wind
that drifts in   unseen

dripping sweat off of lovers
who swell in the morning
orange and brown seeping down
rising again with spring water

night   drown with ebony a
dark   dark green

what is this move to nature
retrieving rock people   fir and marmot
from human history

sealing off history
the usurpation by the born
  from the unborn
the child in suspension

closing off history from not history
a line that is not a line
but nevertheless must not be breached

we recognize our wild breathing
as a membrane that is permeable
both   ways
but only so much so

shed history like a gown that holds
flesh in place

shed it like a skin
the mind is wrapped in
release through it
time and timeless are not in the play of opposites

time extends into timeless
inside of time forever
  inside of timeless

ground squirrel burrows into forest floor

raven carries void through pine canopy

big cat stalks its prey
forest takes back the carcass

history   buried under wings moving

who are the wild brothers and sisters
that history cannot grasp
cannot put to a test   cannot
house in books or exquisite computer graphics

that history cannot walk through

young man lays down on granite rock
dissolves into particles
of
    light   dancing
        figures

young woman emerges
cave dweller
squats in deep meadow
well before   mid day

brown bear stands on hind limbs
converses with grandfather and grandmother

    thousands   of   years
                      ago

Void

Here it comes a rollin' of the void you can hear it
Joy comes as well see how it does that with a word
Singin' starts it then music from her room
Then dancing crazy like
Out of the darkness out of the shadows showing her
If the tempo is right and the turning and the subtle mix
You can get a little crazy with her you two together
But you wait gone taken away somewhere you did not know
There it is maybe just there ready to go the dancing is ready
When it sweeps you then the first
And there you are gone in the night a piece of light
Vanishing into a warm patch of the fully dark
A last and beautiful look
That luminous dark.

Feedback and Feedforward

Body/mind/ecological-awareness relies on the involvement of an individual with their own complex of body signals. It moves along in a particular manner. Utilizing feedback and feedforward as a learning experience, leads to a greater understanding of how the body/mind interaction works.

Negative feedback decreases responsivity and increases control. Positive feedforward increases the gain and the responsivity of the system but places control on a fine edge. It is valuable to recognize the importance of using feedback to test for a feedforward system. Negative feedback acts to inhibit behavior and gain control prior to a goal having been located. Once control has been established a goal must be realized, the behavior can then be aligned with it, feedforward of a positive nature will loosen the control, increasing the momentum towards the goal.

In the beginning feedback would be confusing, it would then be perceived as negative and would lead to a gaining of control over the system as the variability of the feedback response was decreased and stability achieved (S1) (see diagram Appendix 1). At the same time this would manifest as characteristic unresponsiveness, low arousal. Once this state (S2) is achieved then the perception of the feedback signal would change to positive (feedforward) if and only if the achieving of a desired new state (S3) could be seen as being possible as an advent of altering the signal presented by the feedback. If S3 cannot be realized feedback and feedforward would cycle back to S2 in an internal loop that would eventually stop the seeking. This process, that of altering the signal toward a goal, is a discrete state (S4) and is complete once the state has been achieved (S5). Finally the goal has been achieved and the process is complete and ready for the next move.

S1 would be characterized by frustration, lack of understanding, lack of control, attempts to control, ambivalence, and active introjection. S2 would be characterized by a low arousal, relaxed state that will indicate that changes have begun. S3 would of necessity be an active search for this new state with attempts to both articulate the state and gain some experiential insight into it and into its value. The process will shut down at this point if a goal of value cannot be articulated. S4 then is the discrete state within which a depth of experience is obtained to allow one to entirely submerge oneself in the new state. It again is characterized by experimentation, trial and error, feedback and feedforward, and alterations of the state itself. S5 is the completion realized in some significant form and presented in some significant manner.

The entire process is completed at this point and can either be accepted for what it is without introspection (V) much as one might see an opera and not be concerned about what it takes to produce it; or the process can be seen as a unitary experience (Vision) were the various parts lead out of necessity to this the final objective, yet it will be more than the experience, standing as it were, on the foundation of what preceded it but not dependent on what proceeded it. It is not dependent because it has moved one to a condition where what came before can no longer sustain the new state. This is the state referred to in the section Necessity of Strong Support as the state of full "body eco-awareness" where information is an indicator of a matrix of natural internal and external states.

(See Chart of Feedback and Feedforward in Appendix 1)

Attitudes Towards Health

The prevailing attitudes toward health held by the main stream health care industry and the wholistic community leads to particular modes of behavior for the practitioner and the person seeking improvements in health on the level of individual health problems and on the level of over-all health. But always it is important to seek the underlying experience that is the foundation for a satisfying life and constantly strive to hold that in the forefront of our purpose.

From the stand point of the practitioner, health is an area of study, a discipline, a career that is often separate and distinct from other aspects of one's life. Health in all its various elements has become such a convolution of particulars that it seems that to maintain it one must dedicate an inordinate amount of one's life to it. It is as if in order to maintain health one must become a member of the health community and dedicate one's life to health instead of having health as a given starting point for those other significant aspects of one's life. For those who choose this dedication as a guide in the journey to a healthy life it is a laudable commitment. For others there seems to have occurred such a separation of categories of life that even those areas that should form the absolute necessary conditions for life have been separated out and made into either a professional area that only those who have attained a learned level of competency can enter and hence, in the area of health, gain health; or health has become an area that a lay-person must be willing to dedicate extraordinary amounts of time, intellect, money, and attention to in order to have it.

It is possible to get books on health, attend classes, lectures, all manner of workshops etc., to gain and maintain this thing we call health. It is true that all of these things can be done and more until again the gaining and maintaining of health becomes a full time occupation worthy of advanced degrees. It can become a continuous circuit where that substratum of health that is, I contend, primary as a basis for a significant and satisfying life may become more elusive.

It is possible to make a career out of one small part of the stupendous mass of particulars that is this thing we call health or medicine or healing and it is not in this area that I wish to dwell. I give this area over to the researchers and the compilers to sort out and catalogue and come up with the various compendiums that comprise the list of attributes that constitutes health. Instead I will attempt to catch a glimpse into that region that can hold the compendiums no matter who compiles them and through the mostly mysterious process of mind can allow this or the other compendium to be the substratum that underpins the effective life whether or not the individual is aware of all or even any of the parts that may at one time or another comprise it.

Most ideologies have a core vision that entails much of the particulars of that method of organization:

> Plato's Ideal: speaking of his Republic: "Our aim in founding the state was not the disproportional happiness of any one class, but the greatest happiness of the whole; we thought that in a state ordered with a view to the good of the whole we should be most likely to find justice." [20] Islamic Heaven: "The highest level is the seventh heaven, in which God can be seen and where anything is possible." [21] The Modern Hippocratic Oath: from the oath; "I will remember that I remain a member of society, with special obligations to all my fellow human beings, those sound of mind and body as well as the infirm. If I do not violate this oath, may I enjoy life and art, respected while I live and remembered with affection thereafter. May I always act so as to preserve the finest traditions of my calling and may I long experience the joy of healing those who seek my help." [22] The Communist Ideal; "Ideas for how the capitalist society of the time would eventually be replaced by socialism, and then eventually communism." "The falling away of the state." [23] Nirvana: profound peace of mind that is acquired with moksha (liberation).[24] In shamanic thought, it is the state of being free from suffering. In Hindu philosophy, it is union with Brahman

(Supreme Being).[25] *Augustine's City of God: "The peace of the celestial city is the perfectly ordered and harmonious enjoyment of God, and of one another in God."* [26]

Or any other such idealized state or condition that exists if not exactly outside of humanity then at least outside of the explicit conscious moment to moment quality of mind but is nevertheless that which acts moment to moment to give a substratum of effective structure and function to a person's life.

After some time in my study of biofeedback a recognition occurred that altered the content of my thinking. In the beginning the study was into altered states of consciousness as exemplified by the alpha state, this being a state that allowed an integrating to occur that affected relaxation and attention. Yet it became clear that healing and learning were in all cases preludes to some subsequent activity. That activity entered the realm of doing and in that doing something was separated from the state of consciousness that alpha produced. It constituted a distinct move from the internal to the external, engendered movement and required a vision. Here in the vision was to be located the symbolic forms that would galvanize the organism toward a goal do to the actual effect of the symbol on the psycho-physical function.

It was not necessary, as biofeedback had been postulating, to have conscious control, this was only an interesting diversion. What was important was to move to the level of symbols that would, through their effect on systems allow the organism to move in the desired manner. Mircea Eliade in *The Sacred And The Profane*, recognized the significance of symbols to carry the most important of humanity's experiences, in this case acts of manifestations of the sacred (hierophanies). Symbolism *"is the only system capable of integrating all of the particular revelations of innumerable hierophanies. This law, moreover, holds for every symbolism; it is the symbolism as a whole that valorizes the various significations of hierophanies."* Or any important act. Symbols *"reveal their deeper meaning only to the extent to which the structure of (the) symbolism is known."* [27] This is equally true in the sacred area of health.

It seems then that the brain through symbols can carry this thing we call health throughout the organism. But what of these symbols and what of the messages that they carry and what of the conditions that they bring to the organism? Since we are such a symbol laden culture it would be fair to ask what effect symbols have had on our fragile organism. Is our health of a quality to be applauded? Do we act from a substratum of health that is high in quality and basically hidden or do we suffer from maladies that we cannot account for given the "advanced state" of our cultural form? Certainly most of us would answer no we do not as a whole carry a high state of health. Ill health is significant, high health is rare, most fall between and we maintain health at a level less than optimum. And so it might be said that the symbols of this culture carry little in the way of health and much that is of lesser value.

We must go back to the idea, the mechanism whereby an ideal is carried through a vision and how that idea carries the parts that make up a complex symbol.

An ideal we recognize as a form that exists, such as Plato's Ideal, outside of us that we call upon to give significance to particulars that we encounter. An example is a beautiful vase. For Plato this ideal of beauty exists in the world of forms and we draw on them as we recognize beauty. This ideal gives rise to ideas of beauty that we utilize as a rapid set of filters to tell us that this vase is beautiful. Extending from Plato these are not ideas that we gain from our commercial surrounding, though these too may enter, as may ideas that come from home, school, community, peers. This ideal is more persuasive and comes from a source that is the way we are connected (in our view) into the ecological scheme of things. It is the idea of our mind/body/ecological-awareness and how that gets put together, a harmonizing of the various elements of our psyche. We know these ideals at a level of intuition once we have followed the pattern of the organized thought and behavior within the system we are operating in. That is, the ideal is both the result of the symbols and systems and the goal or objective. They become one and the same as we deepen our involvement and further our exploration into that which constitutes the reality (field) that we are involved with. By carefully utilizing particulars from a set of ideals, piecing them together in symbols that are loaded in forms of information and are specific in terms of their effect within the organism, change or behavior can be induced.

> Mircea Eliade says that "the celestial sacred remains active through symbolism. A religious symbol conveys its message even if it is no longer consciously understood in every part. For a symbol speaks to the whole human being and not only to the intelligence." [28]

In the first quote he is speaking to the meaning (compendium), here he is speaking to the whole human being and not only to the intelligence.

We are now approaching health. We have touched upon behavioral change and potential manipulation of internal conditions. We have not yet touched upon health because we have yet to achieve the condition where health exists, as it were. To recognize where we must go we need to realize that a number of things are not the case; first of all we assume that health can be learned, it cannot; second that doing is the objective of a life, it is not; and third that health is privileged to those who can achieve some significantly exalted state, it is not. Finally that health is an objective set of conditions that science and their priests, medical scientists, can delineate and lay out as a set of premises to live by; this is not true and yet it is as valid as any other of the set of ideals that I mentioned earlier.

Let me narrow focus now because the state that is needed is elusive and begs a clear articulation as it should for it is not a reasoned state nor is it poetic, though poetry often gets closer than reason. Health is a state preceding beingness; some have called it unity/love/consciousness/god/spirit/soul. That is it is a condition of existence, a condition in and of itself not privy to analysis nor privy to accurate description; all descriptions are particularizations, all analysis is deconstruction and becomes irrelevant when unity/love/ consciousness/god/spirit/soul is presented. Advanced degrees do not bestow it nor do one more workshop. The closest we can come to it in our intellect and through our reason is in the construction of symbols. I say construction not the use of symbols. The closest we come through poetry and art is in the use of symbols. It is here in Eliade's sense of symbols that so much is revealed that health actually becomes not just possible but a transcending reality. If we recognize ourselves as an integral part of the universe it can only be that what we call health is at the center of what we and the universe are. We come to this because we and the universe are the same, here there is no distinction.

The closest we come before we have it is in movement and dance and most significantly in music. But when we have it we have it and the rest is an approach. So what then is the point of all this? When we have it we have it, we need nothing, no reason, no symbols, no poetry, no music, just it. Yes, this is true, just it and the recognition that a precise set of symbols articulated bring within their sway all the compendiums that make up the diversity and set up the conditions for entrance into life's reality. When special attention is directed to unity/love/consciousness/god/spirit/soul where all the particulars lead, so that each particular roots in unity/love/consciousness/god/ spirit/soul and leads to health, where each compendium roots in unity/love/god/spirit and is a substratum of health, health then is unity/love/consciousness/god/spirit/soul.

Where learning leads not in circles on to itself but to a point where the jump from the cliffs is possible, into a future that is always a mystery, one can stand in a place of truth. Where assumptions are stripped away that degrees and privilege engender great being because unity/love/consciousness/god/spirit/soul is before being only. And finally that one compendium or another gives an exclusive road to truth since unity/love/consciousness/god/spirit/soul, as we have noted, does not depend on the method that is used to approach it.

Lastly it is important for those who are the dispensers of health to make articulate the points on the map to unity/love/ consciousness/god/spirit/soul for those lost in the labyrinth of ill health so that freedom from the confines of the journey can be experienced. Apollo is the god of medicine and he is the spirit of unity as well. Unity in Taoist language is *like the fish swimming in water as the human swims in Tao*. It is a condition and when the condition exists health is a given and then true action indeed can be achieved, life can be lived fully.

(See Alpha Nap exercise in Appendix 1)

circle of wind

tree trunk and bone   leaf mold and wind

this wind is pervasive
there is wind in my thinking   wind in the
incense cedar

my thoughts and yours have wind and tree
holding them skyward
holding them to ground

wind in circles
circling tree trunks
circles of hands holding

tree   wind   bone and leaf

Contemplative Passages

The following passages are contemplative pieces. They are best read before bed, or first thing in the morning, or while sitting outside in the afternoon, or around a fire in the evening. Read the passage over three times. The first time read in your mind for meaning—does this make sense; the second time read in your heart for feeling—what is my response to it; and the third time read in your belly for your instinctive reaction—how does this connect with me on a deep, primal level.

After having read the passage three times let the passage sit with you, don't do anything particular, just be with it and be conscious of what is occurring as this passage sits in your full body/mind/eco-awareness. If appropriate you may wish to write down your response.

A wholistic state

is a state of pure consciousness.
A point where no point of view is taken,
a state where the balance of awareness,
feeling, and instinct
can be experienced in harmony.
A wholistic approach recognizes that a person
is a fully integrated being,
all aspects being no more than arbitrary,
functional, and consensus descriptions
of the person for the sake of interaction
and for the sake of the person living
their particular life.
A wholistic healing state
has far reaching
implications
because if one maintains this healing state
long enough
one will obtain a condition of health
capable of creating in oneself
an aesthetically,
exquisite condition.

The physical body

is the world of the senses.
The means of enhancing the physical body
is to activate the senses fully,
flooding the physical body
with just the right kind
and amount of sensation.
Included in this flooding process is food from the natural
world, music, dance, the full spectrum of color from the
seasonal round
all appropriate to maintaining an internal
condition of balance.
Done with the right attention
a physical body with a sensory
mode of consciousness
would be a vital and fully intact organism.
A base would be laid down that would underlie
all other activity.
Nature as the source of the sensorial world
lays down the deeply
sensual body

In a healthy organism

one's personality acts as a conduit
for the manifestation of higher, more complex
and intricate forms of one's essential nature
mixed with the subtle energies of the
earth/universe currents.
This possibility is mediated
through some form of mastery.
At this level of function there is no blockage,
only a conscious shifting of the appropriate
creative energy towards a consciously
chosen end that is mixed in equal parts
with the mystery of the outcome.
Here it is important not to push
or force the organism
but to allow what is to occur to occur.
Force at this point can lead to a break
in the creative process.
A healthy organism with an intact personality
interacts with the natural world
and performs a creative dance
relating perceptions, feelings, and ideas
into a culturally significant expression.

From an objective point of view

the utilization of energy
through a specific structure
yields whatever result conforms
to that structure,
the result's value is irrelevant to the process.
It is a technology independent of the
potential of its use.
Independently a discussion of values
must be pursued
to establish an answer to the question
of whether the result will be
towards life or away from it.
If at any time it is determined
that some manifestation of power
is being used in a manner that is away from life
then it is the duty of an individual
to withdraw energy
from that expression
and to allow the matrix to run down
due to a lack of continuous
input of energy and attention.

True health

manifests as an organism in balance,
in homeostasis.
It is the basis of all further behavior;
it is the foundation of subsequent living.
Wholistic health includes a feeling of totality,
a recognition of the intrinsic value of oneself,
the awareness of one's relationship to life,
to nature,
to the universe,
to others.
A wholistically healthy condition ties into a
single source
(it is the ground)
and that source is love.
The essence of a human being is fed by love
and will grow as love is given
and love is accepted.
And so we work towards a wholistically healthy state
when we feed the essence with love,
with pure life.

Dream

The dream did not have definite content, rather it
was abstract, more a feeling dream where something
true is sent on a knowing level directly into the
understanding by sending an experience
that is also a statement without words.
It was this: sound or music or words
come and go in all directions
and dimensions, they exist
everywhere all at once,
they are non-localized
where light is generated
from a single source
and is focused.

To forget Man Is Born In Tao

Fishes are born in water
Man is born in Tao.
If fishes, born in water,
Seek the deep shadow
Of pond and pool,
All their needs
Are satisfied.
If man, born in Tao,
Sinks into the deep shadow
Of non-action
aggression and concern,
He lacks nothing
His life is secure.

Moral: "All the fish needs
Is to get lost in water.
All man needs is to get lost
In Tao."

Chung Tzu
From The Way of Chuang Tzu
by Thomas Merton

The challenge is thus

Can we go more completely
Or have we gone as far as can be

If we have surveyed the whole   what now
Can we answer that question
Or are we dedicated to the endless pursuit
No matter the cost

But once we say   whole   it is now   one
And all goes on

Healing the Planet
Part II

wilderness in the city

the place where possum and skunk walk
where hawk circles and cries out

where winter clouds overcome
the reputation of beach and sun

a small spread of blue
the slightest touch of a breeze

everything else asphalt and steel
rough side of buildings and planted trees

nothing made before the first necklace
of fertile beads chipped from black rock

and flung out at the wild creature that
would join the wild creature within

making a looping circle   recognition of cycles
the goddess without voice
here before all this asphalt and steel

Wilderness

"The Wilderness is by no means chaos, it is most
admirably ordered, and organized, quietly and
beautifully obeying the laws of nature."
Wilderness and the Search for the Soul of Modern
Man, by C.A. Meier [1]

"accepting that human control is perhaps not all
that it would like to be, and that we are but a small
part of something far greater." From the forward by
Robert Hinshaw to A Testament to the Wilderness,
Ten Essays on an address by C.A. Meier (Daimon
Verlag, Zurich: 1985) [2]

In the psyche, as in the natural world, in order to affect a
deep and permanent healing, there is a need for wilderness,
the need for a place which operates by laws that are both unmade and
unknown to the inhabitants. We may call these natural laws but that
begs the question because the assumption here is that there are such
laws that are the organizing principles of nature but they are
unrecognized, for to recognize them would be to step outside of nature
and hence lose wilderness. Wilderness then is synonymous with action
inside the laws of nature without recognition and without a loss of
consciousness either. Here is where the homeostatic mechanisms of
nature are that give nature such a power to heal itself. The destructive
and at the same time curative quality of a wild fire is a dramatic
manifestation of this deep mechanism.

Obviously these laws are unmade in the legislative sense.
They are also unmade in any cosmic sense and they are not discoverable
in any scientific sense. They are discoverable, but at the moment in
which they become distinct and observable, wilderness disappears.
These laws appear at the precise moment when the ability to perceive
them is entirely irrelevant because the moment of their perception is
the moment which presupposes their irrelevancy both in order to have
wilderness and, as it were, operate inside it. That is, it is impossible to
be in wilderness and follow the laws that operate there and it is

impossible to recognize laws of nature and be in wilderness. Our eco-awareness operating as instinct keeps us and nature in tune. Consider that moment when the mountains and sky come together inside and the reality is a feeling, a raising of hairs on the skin surface, a cascading of sensation along nerves and a movement of color in the groin; nothing but the experience is there, wilderness as the interior and exterior in the same place. At the moment of observation, at the detailing of "scientific laws," the observed and the observer come into being and wilderness ceases because wilderness is a unitary phenomena and does not exist in the psyche or in nature in separation.

It may appear that a discussion of laws and wilderness would be mutually exclusive and that laws and wilderness would even be anathema to one another. In our social dialogue we equate wild with lawless as in our talk about a wild street gang, or a wild party, or a wild person who is insane or crazy. We tend toward the notion that laws are points of governance and determine behavior because they are either restrictive or they are descriptive and logical corollaries, that, by their understanding, we can alter, manipulate, or in some way augment what it is that they predict or control.

The objective of observation and codifying the laws of nature turns on the desire and the possibility of manipulating them and thus one is automatically outside of nature. This flies in the face of our assumption that we can learn a set of laws/principles etc. and then with this body of knowledge enter the game and hence more fully participate in it. This is true of a game but wilderness is not a game, it is a state of existence. Something is left out of this kind of inquiry and we won't even know that it is left out.

Scientists, and poets may want to take issue with this view. But this is not a demeaning of the discipline the scientist and poet has taken on. Poets and scientists both are fully aware that their discipline is not the thing itself, but rather is a tool for either understanding, and hence affecting the world—the scientist; or understanding and presenting the world—the poet. The hunter may know the reality of the wild best because to most fully find the kill the hunter needs to release to a place of instinctive connection and operate from there; this is true of the best wilderness poetry and may also be true of the most insightful scientific work.

I remember a professor in a dendrology course (the study of trees) years ago, out in the field sitting with the class and having a discussion of the various elements that make up a tree. Roots, trunk, branches, leaves, nutrients drawn up from the earth through osmosis, sunlight transformed into chlorophyll. And then he asked what held it all together, what connected all the elements, and as we recognized the cellular connection throughout we left the scientific discussion and with a look, entered the full unitary consciousness of the wilderness surrounding us.

How then has the degradations of nature and the illness of the body come about and how are they connected?

The idea behind the God-King as exemplified by the Grail story is instructive. Part of the grail story derived from early Celtic traditions that blessed the leader, recognizing that the health of the land was related to the health of the leader. If the God-King was in touch with the land and acted accordingly not only was the land productive but the people as well were healthy and well provided for, the land would provide. The land, the people, and the God-King were all connected. If the God-King became ill or acted improperly it impacted the land and the people as well. Something was out of balance. But what was out of balance, nature? That might be like saying love is out of balance, what could that possibly mean? In geologic time it is even hard to talk about being out of balance as the forces of nature move at such a pace. But what about the God-King or us?

Arthurian legends and the grail may be based to some extent on Celtic lore. The Holy Grail might well have been developed from references to magic cauldrons that appear in many Celtic myths and practices. In her book *From Ritual to Romance* (1920), Jessie Weston [3] traced some similarities between Celtic myths and grail legends. Some Celtic fertility rituals, for example, were designed to ensure the health and vigor of a community leader: the physical welfare of the land was connected with that of the king. The silence and sterility of the Fisher King in a tale like Parzival, then, would indicate some transgression and physical failure of the king that affected his land. Celtic legends have references to the Fisher King as the leader of a barren land, referred to as the Waste Land and "the land laid waste." [4]

The condition of the God-King was indicative of the well-being of the whole; this could be said of us as well. Nature becomes our reflecting surface and the degradation we see there frightens us into seeing our own follies. When the God-King failed to maintain balance, forces occurred from the land itself to redress the imbalance and return health to the land and the people. Sometimes this redress is significant. Does this mean that all naturally occurring cataclysmic events are caused by an out of balance populous? No, just as we cannot take credit for the even-tempered weather of Spring, so we cannot take credit for the floods that from time to time visit us. But to assume then that we are not part and parcel of the land out of which we come likewise is untenable.

The place of wilderness, even in our common and ordinary understanding, goes to a place in our psyche that grasps the idea instinctively and leads us to a very fundamental level of being.

Wilderness in our cultural life has too often taken on a romantic place at best and a fearful place at its worst. The romantic aspect has come in large part through our artistic fascination with nature, "primitive" people and the "mysterious" Orient. These romanticized views have their origins in the super-civilized confines of European based ideas of science, society, and religion. We see this expression evident in our fascination with artists such as Gaugin and Van Gogh and in the longing contemporary (Romantic) artists have about natural sensibilities. Likewise the fascination artists have with Oriental spiritual practices is an attempt to find methods to attain the unifying experience that is central to these systems and that seems so lost in Western spiritual practices. The romantic aspect remains as long as we stay separated and only partake of these experiences as an outsider.

The fearful aspect is played out by all those in the culture who play upon the expression of horror, pain, and death that animates much of the unexplored psyche of many people. We see it in film and TV, books, political manipulation, the fear of illness and disease, the chaos of war, social dissolution, and natural calamity; as well as the religious use of hell and Satan as weapons to control behavior. When we equate wilderness with those times where society has broken down and humanity is in crisis, we do the natural world an injustice and allow ourselves to be lead into organizing against the natural world which further alienates us from it.

Certain expressions of horror, pain, and death are based on long standing and deep psychic experiences that get passed from generation to generation where finally the origin of the real experience is lost to continuous irrational but psychically real and historically actual events. Some year ago, my partner, Laurene, told me of the meaning of the children's nursery rhyme *Ring around the rosies*:

Ring around the rosies

Pocket full of posies

Ashes, ashes

We all fall down

It's origins come from the time of the Black Plague in 13th Century Europe. *Ring around the rosies* is a description of the rose colored pock marks on the victim of the Plague; *Pocket full of posies*; the posy flower was put in one's pockets to help cover up the stench of dead corpses; *Ashes ashes* were the ashes of the corpses that were burned to get rid of them; *We all fall down* recognizing that we all will die of the plague. Seven hundred years later we still teach little children this rhyme, as they all fall down at the end. It has been argued that much of modern medical science gained significant headway in the tragedy of that sad time. "The Black Death deserves a place of importance in the story of the history of European medicine because, though change was slow in some areas, it did eventually force a reassessment of all aspects of medicine, one wherein practical medicine received more attention, study, and status." [5]

Experiences of war, starvation, plague, leave scars that live deeply in the psyche and can be and are, enlivened time and time again by various methods of recall. Never-the-less our sense of wilderness both precedes this and we are instinctually drawn to wilderness even when elements of fear remain.

We find wilderness in many places, out there, beyond the civilized, citified human world; on the land that is the dwelling place of animals, plants, and stones. If we go there we stand a chance of finding wilderness in ourselves, of touching and maybe joining with it.

This is an experience we seek even if we don't or can't go out there to the mountains. Sex at certain times finds wilderness, the unitary experience, wild, moist and unknown. The joining of two soulful territories where a great flowing of energy, a great combining of life forces propels both into a vast uncharted region that is somehow so tantalizing and so intriguing that nothing can inhibit the journey.

Drugs can lead to wilderness in particular situations where their use is unencumbered and the intention is worthy. Terence Mckenna in *Food of the Gods*, speaks of the psychedelic experience; "...life lived in the absence of the psychedelic experience upon which primordial shamanism is based is life trivialized, life denied, life enslaved to the ego and its fear of dissolution in the mysterious matrix of feeling that is all around us." [6]

Travel and adventure can be a means. Wilderness in this context is a place where letting go of norms and strictures occur, where we are relieved of the confines of culture and where we don't disintegrate and "lose our life." In fact we can survive, we can get along. Some other set of instincts well up and we are able to navigate but in a place that is unlike our everyday world. We like adventure and travel so much because the known is lifted and we can experience the new, the unknown and live inside it.

I traveled in Nicaragua in 1990 observing the elections there without the language, mostly on my own. I lived for a week with Alexandria and her young family in the northern city of Esteli'. For hours at a time she and I would sit in her partially outdoor kitchen with smoke rising through the slated roof drinking freshly ground dark Nicaraguan coffee from the volcanic soil of the communal coffee plantation in the surrounding mountains. With the coffee ground with el molcajete (pestel and mortar) and boiled in an iron fry pan, richened with thick brown cane sugar taken from the sugar cane outside her window, we would talk about the revolution, our families, the future of Nicaragua, all manner of things close to us. Our understanding through Spanish and English was only sketchy but we found a place we recognized, an emotional, instinctive way to commune and interact. It was so much more direct than words and there was no doubt as to the meaning. Particulars were more difficult but the human contact was so much more real.

Meditation can lead to wilderness and with a subtle rewrite may be seen as its objective. The release of held patterns of response, of internal presumptions through meditation may allow an entrance into a natural place of the psyche. We experience in the energy of a spiritual master the flowing nature that connects us to an instinctively known and longed for place.

The healing experience is an experience of wilderness. We let go of particular routines, we give up, we get rest, veg out, sleep, change our behavior. The sicker we are the deeper need be the healing, the further into wilderness we must go, releasing our everyday behavior until the balance of nature re-balances us to a healthy state. Death may be the ultimate healing and the ultimate wilderness experience.

It is important not to down play the wilderness out there in rocks and trees. This place is primary to our well-being but we must also talk about wilderness of the psyche, the interior, healing, sex, and the mind.

turtle island

buffalo brother   turtle island
    lupine and the
    range of light
expressed in wood   push
with love   the infidel lover   through
the web of land

The ability to live wilderness both psychically and in the natural world involves at least two powerful traits. The first is a strong enough sense of self so that one knows that by relinquishing the social ego nothing will be lost and also that it can be gained again and hence one will be able to function within the social arena. The second trait is one that requires the capacity not to do what one knows one can do and to not feel superior in that action of non-action. Michael Crichton in his book *Jurassic Park* has the mathematician Malcolm observe that scientists have methods to do all sorts of things but they fail to inquire if they should.[7] Here is the question of values.

By exploring the second trait first, light can be shed on the first. Much of the movement to set aside wilderness areas in our natural world is based upon the recognition of the need for "place" that is uncontrolled and it is a movement that is one of the most profound expressions of our cultural life. The legacy that people like Aldo Leopold and John Muir have left is paramount to our health as a people.

In "The Land Ethic", a chapter in *A Sand County Almanac*, Leopold delves into conservation. In "The Ecological Conscience" section, he wrote: "Conservation is a state of harmony between men and land." He noted that conservation guidelines at the time boiled down to: "obey the law, vote right, join some organizations, and practice what conservation is profitable on your own land; the government will do the rest." (p. 243–244) [8]

> Leopold explained:
>
> *"The land ethic simply enlarges the boundaries of the community to include soils, waters, plants, and animals, or collectively: the land."*
>
> *"This sounds simple: do we not already sing our love for and obligation to the land of the free and the home of the brave? Yes, but just what and whom do we love? Certainly not the soil, which we are sending helter-skelter down river. Certainly not the waters, which we assume have no function except to turn turbines, float barges, and carry off sewage. Certainly not the plants, of which we exterminate*

whole communities without batting an eye. Certainly not the animals, of which we have already extirpated many of the largest and most beautiful species. A land ethic of course cannot prevent the alteration, management, and use of these 'resources,' but it does affirm their right to continued existence, and, at least in spots, their continued existence in a natural state. In short, a land ethic changes the role of homo sapiens from conqueror of the land-community to plain member and citizen of it. It implies respect for his fellow-members, and also respect for the community as such."

The importance of leaving land that is unmanaged even though we have the ability to manage it shows a degree of maturity that far out weighs the childish notion that we will be "alright" if only we can control ourselves and our world. Laurens Van Der Post writing in *A Testament to the Wilderness*: "Some of our scientists talk about 'managing wilderness,' and that worries me a bit. It is like saying they want to control revelation. Not one of those scientists could have created the vision of something like wilderness."

Introduction to Salmon: Running the Gauntlet May 1, 2011 on PBS, Nature [9]

The Columbia River Basin once teemed with young salmon heading toward the ocean and mature salmon returning to their home rivers and streams to spawn. Now, many salmon species of the Pacific Northwest are extinct, and thirteen, including the iconic sockeye salmon, are currently endangered. When European Americans arrived in the area 150 years ago, the subsequent growth and change in population severely affected the ecosystems. Over-fishing, habitat destruction, and dam construction contributed to salmon's decline, which led, in the late-nineteenth century, to a new government-sanctioned industry created to restore dwindling salmon populations: hatcheries. Today, salmon hatcheries provide controlled environments where early developmental stages of the salmon life-cycle are replicated within the confines of concrete walls;

73

eggs are artificially fertilized and incubated in tubes and plastic bags, and young salmon are raised in tanks before being released into the wild.

Regrettably, however, those very systems set up with the intention of saving salmon are contributing to the species' devastating decline. The hatcheries' controlled environment strips salmon of the genetic diversity and natural instinct critical for their survival in the wild. Once released into open rivers and streams, these populations of fish are vulnerable to a variety of challenges they are unprepared to meet. Though ambitious efforts have been made to monitor and assist hatchery salmon in the wild – from barge and truck transportation around dams, to predator relocation programs – the results of those efforts have been essentially unsuccessful.

Salmon are an integral part of the ecosystems of the Pacific Northwest. Returning to their spawning grounds, they bring with them nutrient-rich marine nitrogen from the ocean. During their run, they feed all manner of wildlife, including bears and eagles, and they subsequently fertilize the surrounding forests. After they die, their bodies feed countless microorganisms, which in turn feed salmon hatchlings. It remains to be seen if the various efforts of legislators, biologists, engineers, and conservationists can restore salmon numbers, and in the process, restore the vital role salmon play in the health of the land, and in the lives of the animals and people that depend on them.

This recognition of wilderness in the external world has obvious corollaries in our inner world and carries similar consequences. It allows us to not be coerced into organizing our psyche away from those natural elements that constitute wilderness. The need to control and the need to feel protective can lead away from the actuality of wilderness. This does not preclude protecting wilderness, rather it gives us the opportunity not to do even though it can apparently be done. Psychically we are in a similar circumstance. To explain and manage the inner world can likewise be given up to the willingness to be in it without control. Healing is not a controlled behavior. It is a mechanism of balance, of releasing to the balancing forces found most readily in nature, in the wild. The dream is a beautiful manifestation of this "giving in."

The dream gives us access to the unencumbered place where judgment is suspended and our psyche flows according to natural laws without interference from ego or social strictures. The high, lucid dream can be enlightening; the chaotic (normal) dream confusing but revealing; and the dark, moist dream (often mistakenly called a nightmare) can be deeply enlivening. Learning the lesson of the dream also requires the suspension of the critical mind and asks a willingness to be with the dream and partake of its wisdom.

Looking at the first trait, relinquishing the social ego, now takes on more significance. The willingness to release selfhood or personal ego, which is powerfully associated with culture, and rightly so, will allow a move into and with a part of being that is of great importance to the well-being of a person. It will allow a move to wilderness where other traits, important to our human condition can hold sway. From Mckenna: *"If the ego is not regularly and repeatedly dissolved in the unbounded hyperspace of the transcendent other, there will always be slow drift away from the sense of self as part of nature's larger whole."* [10] Illness has a clear opening if this dissolving does not occurs periodically.

It is not necessary to do this so that one can function better in the social reality. It is not significant as a resource to bring back to personal ego awareness. It is not important to do anything with the experience or to expound on its loss or its virtues. What is important is the thing itself. This by itself will preclude the infringement of the non-wilderness. It becomes a willingness and a surrender where the reality itself is sufficient. What comes of it is a question without content. Nothing is determined and nothing is lost as well.

The place of wilderness in the landscape of the country is vital and provides a refuge to which we can go but, it is not enough to ensure that characteristic of being that we need to maintain our integrity as human creatures. The wilderness of our psyche is equally part of the challenge and if recovered could do much to insure the wilderness of landscape.

In preparing some poetry for a performance at Yosemite National Park's Centennial Celebration in 1990 I wrote about my sadness upon learning that a micro-organism, introduced by humans, had made the water, even in the high country, undrinkable without treatment. "Either we have begun the inexorable process of degrading this place or it has come to regard us as a menace and may well be creating an environment to shoo us away, expelling us from the place we once so mystically shared." In the balance of nature we may be seen as the agent responsible for the imbalance. In nature's response to this imbalance we may need be the element lead to extinction. Nature's response to our lack of consciousness may be leading it to flee from us, removing as it does the foundation of our frantic constructions until they crumble and return to the stones from which they came.

There is a way in our psychological space to stay aware, stay conscious without succumbing to the acculturated fear that drives us to separate and look for the danger out there and inside. When one accepts the many manifestations of consciousness, and that of course includes the consciousness of nature, it becomes possible to move about with images and connections that are effortless. Within, without, the trees and rocks are equal with the daily activity, with the car and the supermarket, everything is full of consciousness and nature is not denied. It need not be conquered and subdued, not made to conform to this or that. Recognizing one's ground in the natural world becomes a source point of consciousness. Not to understand, not to utilize, but to accept and become. Being aware, conscious, we can act in accord with the "laws of nature," inside the wilderness out there, the wilderness in here, in the dream that erases the line between.

*The seat of the soul is where the inner world
and the outer world meet. Where they overlap.
It is in every point of the overlap*

Novalis[11]

Dream

Waiting to go through a gate to get on an
airplane going to a conference. The gate
and tickets were a blue green. There is an old building
inside the gate with 3 or 4
apartments. In one lives a poet who is well known. At
first he is old, then young. The building
is 100s of years old.
Tom, a poet friend, and I go in.
Tom recedes to the background, remaining
a presence. I introduce myself. There are others
in the room, young women and men.
The poet mentions my work, I am a bit amazed, but I
understand what he's referring to.
He then goes on to speak of my work in reference
to his latest book. He opens his book and begins
to read. Soon the words disappear and there are large
blocks of orange and brown colors
moving across the page in an organic motif,
much like a mountain scene but more abstract.
He reads these organic abstractions, sometimes
hesitating, unsure of their meaning,
going on to others whose
meaning is clearer until
they become smaller and smaller with an almost infinite
number, their meaning is more
and more difficult to interpret into words.
I understand his point and pick up his book,

it is laid out in word poems
but in a blocked out style on the page.
Later I go off to a very large black room
and the same words and organic abstractions
are arranged on the huge wall. I walk past them, to other
motifs that show up like large purple patterned Indian
bed spreads with large blocks of magenta, ochre, and
forest green lined
with narrow bands of reddish brown and teal figures.
I feel that I am getting closer
and closer to some very primary elements.
Devon, my son, comes into the scene and I
move back to the poet's room and we exchange
awareness of what happened.

For All Blue Canyons *

*"Many Marchers said they had awoken
from consciousness to find butterflies
fluttering about their lips.
Some even believed they had been dead
drowned, and that the butterflies had
brought them back to life."
- from Satanic Verses by Salmon Rushdie*

Yes, this is a fine place.

*The D-13 caterpillar blade howls into the deerbrush
bursting it from the ground like a boil exploding
the blue atmosphere stained with diesel smoke
a dark acrid haze.*

*Nothing here, no great Black Oak, Bull Pine,
no fresh mountain water
diving into granite pools.*

*400 eighteen wheelers roll on the head of coyote
its continuous yelping causing eardrums
to vibrate like a child screaming.*

*Canyon slopes are ripped open sending dust clouds
over the eyes of astronomers and tourists
until we can't see trash disappear
into metaphorical land fills.*

*Neighbors given a free pass to watch 3 million
tons of garbage heap up; old bicycles, vases broken,
frayed chairs, rotting food, plastic containers,
bottle upon bottle, Campbell soup cans line the canyon
walls in place of buckbrush, bottlebrush and sage.*

Ansel Adams' eyes open, John Muir comes awake.

3 Million people line the canyon slopes with dust
covered eyes, ears vibrating to the diesel motor,
blood satiated with acrid smoke, throwing
arms and legs into Caterpillar graves.

Near the roadside a single orange monarch butterfly
moves across the canyon, her wings at first tiny
as they beat in the blue air, then become huge
as they envelope the whole canyon.

*Blue Canyon in San Diego County proposed as a new trash
dump was defeated by local protest.

Coyote's Complement

Brandon Cesmat, John Peterson, Chris Sullivan

Coyote trots among oaks
burrows into a trash can;
whatever the difference the
terrain matters not as knowing the predator.

As coyote walks up the driveway
she sights the stray
chasing it down the sidewalk,
yipping until she swallows...

***

Indoors his wife waits
with a warm dinner.
He hurries home as
quick as traffic will allow.

Headlights shine
across the lawn to
coyote,
lithe from an uneven
diet of runaway
house cats and poodles.

"Go on!" he shouts.
She lopes across the street.
He has a wonderful view of her
scrambling down the canyon.

Coyote's haunches creak
consciously, her weight
shifting foot to shoulder,
shouldering calm space,

looking back,

tracing lines down hills covered by
black oak and poles encased in creosote,
low-pressure sodium lights and sage,

paw prints on soft sand down
eroded creek banks and roadside
shoulders crumbling to nothing.

Wind whispering "dust, dust"
precedes him up the driveway.

The man looks sideways
perceptions released
as the evening news disappears.
Never read, though he knows
himself and remains true to
his plate glass point of view;
coyote gazes and leers
at him cocooned on the lawn
of his orchestrated chaos.

***

"The Indians were fools," he says,
"Indians were?" she asks.
"Are. Look at the property they let go."

From the backyard they survey
the terrain of the neighborhood
"Fine work, fine work."
"Without us it's just desert."
On the lawn, sprinklers hiss
like static. "Fine work."

***

To her, his wife,
his mate,
wilderness, sounds of
mowing grass and melancholy,
reminds her...
something less soothing
than affordability.

"We are the predecessors;
and we see them, you and I

(don't we?) in one
another?

Apprehensions of
beyond
mowed grass and malnutrition
confronts us as in a mirror;
and we reflect
you and I
(don't we?) one
another.

The panoramas
we share are present and
take precedence
regardless of our bond to him,
despite our debt to predecessors."

Coyote and woman muse
on a horizon now lodged
and vanished beyond
tree tops and humming wire.

"Without this desert there
is just us," coyote whispers

And man and woman whirl
in desert wind,
wild creature on
arm hairs and cocked
head

Coyote's world
over and over.

***
She yips and howls at the night:
sounds like someone singing to him,
keeping him awake.

He encounters wilderness
every day: lawn to mow,
skunks run-over in the road.

***

It wasn't that coyote spoke
English; she did not
but he at last listened
"Where do you think you live?
water rationed, traffic jammed,
crowded schools, your tires slashed?
You live in wilderness, man."

Coyote silences her singing to eat.
Woman lulled to sleep beside him,
his soul leaning against his spine,
the paws of the world on his chest....

Wilderness in the City

As we look for a means of repairing the break between nature and culture, the psychic as well as the physical break, we eventual find ourselves up against a peculiar situation. We find that everywhere we turn, nature and the wild jumps out at us and we find that we must recognize and find wilderness inside that greatest bastion of our defense against the onslaught of nature—the city. To recognize wilderness inside our cities requires a different kind of approach, a different set of perceptions. The creation of natural oases in the cities, such as Golden Gate, Balboa, or Central Park, though they are fundamentally important to our well being as inhabitants of cities, they are not the solution. And it is not the wildness, or rather the skirting of the law, of gangs, rebellion, or pop music culture that generates a certain exciting image of life outside the social norms that gives this sense of the wild. Rather it is instead a way of recognition, a way of thinking and a method of perception that leads to a way of being inside what now passes for cities. And this is not a plea to accept what is happening in cities and just see some romanticized image of nature placed over the often dehumanized aspect of cities cleaved off and alienated from the land out of which they grew. Changing our perception of where we live will change not only ourselves but our surroundings.

Some years ago I took on an extended exercise in changing perception while living in San Diego, a city that is set amongst carved canyons, mesas, and mostly dry river beds. Through foresight on the part of the community much of the canyon lands have remained intact and are off limits to development. And through lack of foresight, heavy development occurred in the Mission Valley area around the mostly dry San Diego River. Dry except during the few heavy winter storms when the river floods and creates havoc with the excessive development. I lived near Balboa Park and while making a concerted and long term effort to recognize the elements of nature and the wild, began to see and experience a very different city.

The city was full of wild creatures, possum, skunk, fox, and further out coyote. The mildness of San Diego's weather became a subtle barometer of changes where even the smallest adjustments in temperature became cause for excitement. At this time it was disconcerting to recognize areas where nothing remained of the natural landscape. In parts of the city nothing was visible but concrete, asphalt, buildings, cars and spits of planted grass and trees. Still, training one's perceptions to see nature and the wild was extremely enlivening. Certainly the proximity of the ocean in a place like San Diego enhances the opportunities to approach the wild.

It is curious that one of the first things we do no matter the level of our success is to return to the wild. We may purchase a cabin in the mountains, a house in the country, buy a boat to motor or sail the lakes or oceans. Quite out of instinct we seek and find a return to Mother Earth and Mother Ocean, to reconnect and nurture us. And yet this is mostly not available to the economically modest or disadvantaged.

I worked at one time for the Forest Service in the Palomar Mountain area of San Diego County in a Youth Conservation Program and was both amazed and shocked to find 16, 17, 18 year old youth who had never been out of their city environment; some had never been off the few blocks around their home.

It seems important that we find a way of returning us and the cities to the ultimate source of our being no matter our economic condition.

One move that will have to be made to assist this return is to distinguish between laws that have usurped the life of the city and those laws of the wilderness that underlies the wild itself. We'll also need to learn how to move our perception so that we see the wild that is before us. And we'll need to find a way to bridge the gap between the city and the wild and be with nature without fear, without romanticism, because this is a necessary condition of our well-being. Finally we'll need to release the method of attainment, releasing so that we can be with the natural world that surrounds us even in the city.

Basho's Pond

*(from a recording of music based on the teachings
of Bagwan Sri Ragnesh - Osho)*

*Today   in the late afternoon
with the sun giving off white rays
and a curious wind blowing
I sit and refocus my perceptions*

*Eyes removed from buildings
and hard surfaces   ears release
cars and the sound of sirens*

*Brain releases city and they all
with a sideways look pick up
the wild flute and guitar   tabla   harp
and tamboura and join the mind and
heart in the seeking of wild*

A strange and peculiar waiting

hearing   *Basho's Pond*

on the edge of
listening

there   *there*

88

in the   date palm

yellow   sun light   swaying

        circular   motion

    wind and   sound   and

     mind

        given   back

            instantaneous

    where   wild   danced out

       at me

Wilderness in the City

The place where possum and skunk walk
where hawk circles and cries out

Where winter clouds overcome
the reputation of beach and sun

A small spread of blue
the slightest touch of a breeze

Everything else is asphalt and steel
sides of buildings and planted trees

Nothing made before the first necklace
of fertile beads   chipped from black rock

And flung out at the wild creature that
would join the wild creature within

Making a looping circle   recognition of cycles
*   the goddess without voice*
here before all this   asphalt and steel

One of the pitfalls in a discussion of this sort is that we will not stay in the larger framework, in the macro view, long enough to get at the subject. The danger is that we will want to get into the details of doing, of how to stop growth, how to create more parks, how to find some way to make something happen around this subject. That is all very important but what is needed at some point and on a regular basis is to stay inside the big picture, let go to the rather large notion that indeed cities are already in wilderness. This has always been so and it cannot be otherwise. In this case the details obscure the truth of the proposition. We are already in wilderness.

Some years ago in Fresno I lived in what was called a freeway house. It was one of the many homes that were bought up by Cal-Trans to be demolished for Highway 41, slated to be built in years to come. I lived with my family in a 1/4 mile wide stretch of open land that lay out in front of me for miles. It was a wilderness in the heart of a city that was uncontrolled. Left to its own wildness it was a haven for animals and birds, dogs and humans to run through. I so enjoyed the short time I lived in this free wild place.

This is not to misconstrue wilderness as another catch-all phrase for everything that is, because by wilderness we do not mean something that is a construct of mind and so we have a most difficult time stepping up to it via mind. It can be done but it is difficult at first.

Wilderness first off is a visceral thing and we come to it when we remove the constructs of mind laid over our ancient visceral connections and move into a place very much known but very much shielded from our knowing because of centuries of conscious and then unconscious disconnecting.

Most of us, when first approaching the subject of wilderness, conjure up vast tracks of land without roads or dwellings, inhabited by wild, dangerous animals; lacking in the amenities to sustain our life and visited by the furious elements. Mostly these have been things to fight against, tame, overcome, control, civilize but never succumb to.

Cities have become the bulwark against that in the wild that is overwhelming and dangerous. It is our way of winning the struggle for survival by shutting out the wilderness itself, there-by locking us into the mind-set that sees life as a constant struggle for existence.

Standing on a roadside next to the Kings River in the foothills of the Sierra, I saw a turkey vulture fly towards me low to the ground, maybe twenty feet high. After this great black bird with wide stretched wings and small red head flew by, I watched in awe as it did a complete barrel roll and continued to fly off into the setting sun.

I stood there looking over the lush green fields and I knew then that Winston Hibler, the voice of all those wonderful Disney nature films I remember seeing as a boy, was wrong. It is not about survival in the wilderness, it is about joy, playfulness, excitement and fun. These creatures live inside of the full complement of life, survival being only one element. At that time I was part way into being extracted from books, extracted from a narrow mind-set, so that I could, in myself, recognize a more complete experience of wilderness.

This is not about saving wilderness really, it is not going anywhere. It is about saving us, saving our own lives, saving the cities that we find so attractive and frustrating; flying with that vulture and doing cartwheels in the setting sun. Standing inside of the life that is here, trusting that life and rolling with it without letting the survival part of that experience either disappear or take over.

It is a question of who shapes the world that we experience. If we hold the mind open to experience wilderness in our belly, in our heart, we might just find the way to experience wilderness in our mind, here in the city. From that experience we might be able to write a few lines of poetry that will do it justice and we might help expand a vision that is just the thing itself.

We might begin to breakdown the mentally constructed barrier between city and wilderness and experience them both together, in the same place, here in the city that lies like a hollowed out place etched into the wilderness, connected by lines that reach deep into our past, deep into the lives of the creatures about us.

Towards Sleep

Approaching sleep   not yet deep
animals enter   deer and coyote
possum and coon   raven and jay

They cross the line   that ineffable place
that is protected without our
knowing why

And   all through the night   out there
not in the dream   these creatures
cavort and play   wrestling
in the leaves and running wildly
across the porch at my feet

Four Exquisite Corpse Pieces from Poetry, Meditation and Wilderness Retreats

The first two pieces written in Julian in December by Sylvia, Laurene, Kate, John, Julia, Leslie, Joel, and Sajra

Opening the circle to see what comes

The wind, the cedars, the sun, my friends,
feeling the gifts of the great circle

And we laughed at ourselves and
with each other, warmly and together

But still a long pool of sorrow seems to stretch about me

All of the universe in the
atom flow of one slender pine needle

This wind clears everything, the sky
the mind, the breathing

***
The thoughts that burn like hot embers

Musing on the eternal

Fire fuels friendship, warms my heart

Yes I've been here before, when,

and as I am here trying to let go of past
experience and be in the present, it is hard

The earth folds the great quiet into itself once more

And the raw green wind chills my
flesh and warms my heart as it calls me
back to the place I've always known

***

The second two pieces written on Mt. Palomar by Jack,
Brandon, Priscilla, Sylvia, Miles, John, Michael, and Neyah

"I don't remember," she says,
"ever arguing in front of a fire."

Low and dark and germane
to the moment
A gathering of generations around the
tribal fire weaves the universal stories,

old trails, newly crusted snow, switch back,
break through

The stars twinkle brightly in the frigid moonlit night

This fire at my back, cold at my face exulted

and the ghost ship sinks swiftly in the silent water

This is a fine day now - with the dim light and
a circle of friends around the fire

***

The night and the day are as one in a
world with no timekeepers, and

frigid in the cold night air, I rave

The stories are told and more
stories are remembered and a rhythm emerges

elders propose a spell
lasting longer than any
other known, coming up
hard on a short span

The gentle, strong, wild light of the moon
outside, the drum and the fire inside,
boundaries soften, friends become intimate

The fire crackles brightly in the pale moonlit
night as a meteor passes overhead

Our voices, drum and the hoop of land, the talk
that is our talk, the drum of our life

And the world is wreathed in a corona of fire -
as if it were a funeral pyre

Cold night, new moon, warm old hearts

Wisdom of the Natural World

John Peterson and Jack Seileman

Reprinted from New Vision Journal October 1992

When Albert Einstein was asked what is the most important question a person can ask in his life, he responded, "Is the universe a friendly place or not?" In the present world, with the history that we all share, how can we answer this question?

Some years ago a group of writers met monthly in a year long series entitled, "Poetry, Meditation, and Wilderness." The group, with members changing from month to month, gathered to spend time on the land, to meditate and write with the intention of seeing what was on the inside and what was out there in the wilderness and how they are connected.

At times it became clear how difficult it is for us, coming from our human-centered surroundings, to interact with the natural world. When we first arrived in the mountains on one occasion we congregated in groups, conversing about those things in our lives that matter, that concern us in our day-to-day human reality. For so long we remained unaware of the beings of the natural world around us: rocks, trees, wind and water, animals and birds.

In these times of unrest and breakdown in the city, fear about our environment, and our planetary future, our group went into the wilderness, into the deserts of Anza Borrego, the mountains of the Lagunas, the meadows on Mt. Palomar, and the canyons of San Diego.

We go to the natural world seeking an old understanding that requires us to perceive in a new way. We find that it is not enough just to be on the land. We must be willing to drop the old fears that are based on the competitive fight for survival—the centuries-old perceptions of the natural world that have set us apart from it.

We must be willing to drop the claim, drawn from the still prevalent Biblical view, that the natural world is ours to dominate. We must also see clearly the scientific model that has given us the knowledge to do so many things, but often without a complete understanding of what we are doing.

We find that we must be willing to seek new and often startling relationships. We are beginning to grasp the significance of the old/new paradigm that recognizes the unity of all things and what this means for our own experience, our relationships and our growth.

We may get directions from traditional cultures that are closer to the land, like the need to become less encumbered by our possessions. We may get exacting scientific descriptions of our problems, like the breakdown of the ozone layer and the greenhouse effect and global warming. But what we really need are direct experiences, personal interactions with the beings of the natural world, including the non-human mineral, plant, and animal majority. We need experiences through which we may receive guidance in finding the solutions to the immense problems and large challenges that the outmoded, dominant view toward the natural world have created and continue to create.

John Muir was a clear being who could listen and hear. He said, *"Bend to the persuasion that is flowing to you from every object in nature to be its tongue to the heart of..."* humanity.

A willingness to drop old ways of perceiving and allow for new and unexpected experiences to arise requires daring. While walking through the city streets after the group spent the evening in one of San Diego's many canyons, one member remarked how this was the first time they had walked in the wilderness in the city. The mental barriers between city and country, culture and nature were lowering.

To drop old ways requires a fascination with and a trusting of life, an excitement to what is both new and very, very old, and certainly to what is quite different from our present cultural context. We'll know more the solutions to the problems of our ailing world when we know more about who we are involved with.

As a society we need to seek clarity about what has caused us to become prodigal children of this good earth. It is time to go to the land to shed the civilized, cultural ways and postures that separate and insulate us from the flux of wild, natural life in ourselves and in our world. It is time to end our estrangement from our biological animal self. It is time to show ourselves and the world that we are deserving of our species name, Homo sapiens, "wise primate."

Most of us, especially those of us living in cities, spend much more of our time with our own kind than with our non-human fellow inhabitants of planet earth. We only have each other as our primary role models. We are members of a species that has forgotten ways of being in the world.

The human path and posture is not working. It hasn't worked for a long time. It is one of the primary factors that brought us to this critical juncture in our evolution. Either we come home to who, what, why, where, and with whom we really are or we leave home.

We need to re-open the feedback loops, the lines of communication between us and our wild brothers and sisters, and hear what they say. As a group of writers, one of our exercises was to try and recognize when we were writing about ourselves, when we were describing the world out there and when we were acting as a voice for the beings of the natural world.

> In an essay from Turtle Island called, The Wilderness, Gary Snyder says, "The reasons I am here is because I wish to bring a voice from the wilderness, my constituency...The voice that speaks to me as a poet, what Westerners have called the Muse, is the voice of nature herself, whom the ancient poets called the great goddess, the Magna Mater; I regard that voice as a very real entity."

Our soiled laundry has built up to the point where our "maids and servants" (the oceans, the air, the land) can and will no longer do it for us. We must clean it ourselves.

And so we seek out those who do their laundry regularly, who are clear and clean, light and bright; those who know how to be in the world in ways that add to the overall equality of life on earth: Sun, Moon, Earth, Sky, Hummingbird, Granite, Oak, River, Mountain, Desert.

We come to them with proper posture, humble, loving, respectful. We reach out to them from our ceremonial and ritual circles. We touch them with our prayers for their health and well-being. We ask from our hearts and our bellies for their help, their guidance on our journey home to healed selves and healed relationships with our world.

They come to us, these wild, whole, self-realized sisters and brothers—on the oceans, in the canyons of the city, in the clouds outside our airplane windows. In our dreams and feelings they come to us, ready, willing and able to teach us of truth and integrity, wisdom and balance, beauty and cooperation.

In Doug Boyd's book about Rolling Thunder, a Native American medicine man, he recounts an incident between Alice, an apprentice, and a group of bees.

> Rolling Thunder says to Alice, "If you can talk to dogs that way, you can talk to bees, and they will understand. They won't understand the English language, but they'll understand your meaning just as you say it."
>
> "So he told me what to say to the bees," Alice recounted. "I was supposed to ask (them) to share the plants with me, to tell them I wouldn't harm them, and to explain that I needed the plants for good medicine, but I would leave enough for the bees and for seeds for the coming year. He told me to say it loud and clear.
>
> "I did as he said and, do you know, the bees actually understood me, and they moved! I just can't describe how I felt. All the bees on the plant I was looking at moved. They all moved together to the back of the plant." "I took only the front half of the plant which they had left me, and then I moved to another plant covered with bees, and the same thing happened!
>
> > We are here through
> > all the changes
> > We leave our signs for
> > any who care to see
> > But we do not leave them
> > to be seen

On one of the plants, when the bees moved back and I started to cut, they all made the strangest buzzing sound. It felt as though they were somehow speaking, telling me to stop, and I was understanding.

I looked at Rolling Thunder and he said, 'There now, you see? You and the bees have agreed to share and now you're cutting back too far. They'll expect you now to do as you said.' So I cut only the front half very carefully. Then Rolling Thunder came up to me and he said that this was a gift of the Great Spirit! It is not easy to listen.

We are all mixed up
us and you
How do we know where
the boundaries are
The wind through the hairs
on my arm

It is time for us to find an answer within ourselves to Albert Einstein's question, "Is the universe a friendly place or not?" It is time for people to seek out and surrender to places and postures, beings and experiences that will help the knowing to soak in and seep out - especially in our hearts and bellies - that we live in a world that loves us.

The challenge is intriguing, exciting. "The last frontier is the one that separates (humanity) from the rest of creation," says writer Albert Saijo.

As the barriers come down we are not lessened. We now commune with a greater and greater number of realized beings, the stone and tree, the earth and sky, who carry the wisdom of millennia, a thousand, thousand shamans, buddhas as numerous as the sands of the shoreline, their knowledge, experience and wisdom not to be given, but to be shared so that we all can live fully. It is time to be daring.

If you've got story, heart,
then speak yourself,
stand for it.
- Bill Neidjie, Aboriginal Australian

Tuolumne Meadows -
Adventures in Weather

Reprint from Vision Magazine June 1995

A few years ago our family spent a month camping in Tuolumne Meadows, 9000 feet high in the Sierra Nevada Mountains, the emerald jewel of Yosemite National Park. Camping in the month of June at such an elevation is always a challenge, but the locals said this year was particularly rough. The weather didn't even turn to spring until after the 4th of July. Tent camping in such conditions with a one year old and a three year old becomes a particular adventure.

After driving all day from Palomar Mountain in San Diego County we arrived in Fresno at 5:00 in the evening to pick up the friends who were to accompany us. On impulse we decided to make the four hour drive to the high country that night rather than wait until morning.

We pulled into the Tuolumne Meadows Campground around 10:00. The air was cold, the ground wet and snow covered, and here, after the long drive with young children, the bottom dropped out. This was the wrong place for a family. The thought of putting up a tent was the wrong thought. We stopped, took a deep breath to collect ourselves and bring our thoughts to a more reasonable plan. A tent cabin at Tuolumne Lodge - with a fire - was the right plan, and so we settled in for the night. It turned out we settled in for a few days, cozy and warm, eating meals at the Lodge Dining Room and the Lembert Dome picnic area. It rained and remained seriously cold all week.

We might as well have called this "adventures in weather." In fact at one point we did; this was not a vacation but an adventure and so we operated accordingly, deciding each day if we should continue our stay. Remaining both flexible in our itinerary, as we could not be sure from day to day what we could do, and developing a keenness for the new and unexpected that adventures always bring, we began to settle down. The weather came, all of it; thunderstorms, rain, hail, snow, and cold - serious cold - yes, and a day or two of sun now and then, to which we were thankful.

We moved from the Lodge to a large 6-person tent, tried to say warm and dry with young kids, and deal with the varieties of weather. Clear in the morning, cloudy in the afternoon, rain, clear nights, or some variation, was the mark of each day.

One afternoon, the storm became serious; huge thunder-heads, lightning strikes all over the high country, hail in large quanti-ties, and snow—enough so that the Rangers closed the road on either end of the Meadow. The temperature dropped and we hightailed it for the Lodge for the night. Weather, weather!

Was there anything besides weather? Yes, Devon fell into Tenya Lake, clothes and all; Kiirsti fell off—or into—Lembert dome, skinning her nose; and Laurene was a trooper. We also had some nice hikes in the Meadow, and evenings around the camp fire under the cold clarity of stars.

While talking with Laurene about our eating habits at such a high, cold elevation, it became clear that places, conditions, and activities have a distinct bearing on the kind of consciousness one cultivates. "State specific consciousness" was the term I used several years ago to designate the kind of awareness that revolves around specific circumstances.

Here we eat more, drink hot herbal teas, coffee and Kahlua to warm the interior, and generally bulk up to deal with the rather harsh conditions. Our consciousness extends inward and outward in particular ways. We do focus more on what we call survival or conservation issues, but this is too simplistic. Along with this comes heart concerns for the others in the group, their well-being, comfort, outlook, etc., plus the close camaraderie that occurs when dealing with difficult external conditions. The attention to the surroundings, first dealing with weather and the possibility of rain, cold, snow, etc. turns to a greater appreciation of the beautiful play of wind, clouds, sun, and storm on Mt. Lyell and the surrounding granite peaks.

A cold wind on the face, the power of Lodgepole Pine, Red Fir, Marmot, Sierra Chickaree and the other beings here who deal with these elements year after year, gives us a more pronounced respect for the ability of all of us to adapt, survive, and find the extraordinary no matter where we are. The consciousness out there takes in all of this and more.

During breaks in the rain and snow, and with the proper layered clothing, we find time to enjoy the vigorous wonder of the place. With Devon and Kiirsti tucked in the bike trailer we ride through the Meadow singing our song, "Oh we're riding along, on Tuolumne Road, everywhere that we go(ad) there's another pot ho(ad)." Our rhymes are forced but the exhilaration comes easily. The consciousness that turns inside deals also with issues of well-being, but again this passes as we adapt behavior to the conditions, secure the interior spaces and insure that all will be well. Finally, the interior consciousness curves into old sources, deep historical and primordial places of remembrance; how it was, what the ancestral conditions were. We reflect on the native people who made this their summer home; who trekked the trails from Mono Lake to the Valley floor, bundled up against the changing conditions. Sitting with our hot coffee and Kahlua around the fire after the children are finally wrapped in sleeping bags, we also recall our ancestors, bundled as they were against the harshness of the Scandinavian weather, an ancient fire warming their front, the dark cold night at their back. Their stories are coded still in tissues, cells, memories, and associations. A calmness comes from knowing that we, all of us, have shared these times, human to human over millennia.

Finally the connection, at a core level, of our shared place with the beings of the natural world, Lodgepole, Marmot, Golden Eagle, Junco; we are learning from the inside of their ways, recognizing how closely our lives and theirs are intertwined.

Our respect for the wild world grew in these weeks as did our personal humility. We gained a different sense of what life in the city means. Dealing with small children in such harsh conditions is taxing beyond what is comfortable. We'll enjoy the comforts of our home upon our return to the city. Hopefully our critique of the city, and the rise of industrial and technical development, will, in the future, be more pointed and will not lapse into blanket condemnations with some romanticized vision of living in the wild. The question of how to protect the wild world, and partake in its wisdom remains, as well as how to make the cities more in tune with nature and yet not lose the comforts that cities can bring. We'll come to these questions with more equanimity I think.

We have gained a deeper appreciation for the wildness of the wild, and recognize that we must come to it with our strength intact, meeting it with vigor, preparation, and a mature resolve.

Now, no matter what fire we warm ourselves in front of, this adventure, high in the cold light of Tuolumne Meadows will fill our conscious remembrance. We draw from a submerged, hidden place, set down in this primordial encounter.

hide

*hide inside a tree for awhile
a lodgepole would be ok*

*don't come out 'til the
madness dissolves like*

*snow on the subalpine
meadow*

be sure and ask first

in mountains

lost in mountains
        extracted from books

i'll meet you on the trail
hidden by the bracken fern
and we shall breath

Poetry, Poets,
the Poem and the
Political Process
Part III

When This Generation
-hoffmanoakridge

precisely when this generation
    blindingflash

the moment a single jarring
sets the soul in motion
                    hoffmanoakridge

that common soul that through this
generation moves the apocryphal
moment   synapselightbody

that is the death cold
    shadowbodiesonstonewalls

black as priests robes or god's
immaculate other   expanding
and yes the most inner decision
to survive   yea the only impulse
in it's yet to be foraged history
when it could survive at all
and make a point of light   the
etching of an entire moment
          insideoutside

some precede this moment
      some trail it

some warble on its infinity

Poetry, Poets, the Poem and the Political

If the political process is to be imbibed with the stuff of poetry it seems we as poets and lovers of poetry have a difficult time. Poets have the reputation of being soft, lovers not fighters, dreamers, unwilling and unable to enter the vicious world of politics.

Eugene McCarthy, peace candidate for President in 1968 openly wrote poetry. Jimmy Carter once out of office again openly wrote and published poetry. McCarthy was cast aside in the 1968 run up to the election though he is credited, by many, with opening the Democratic Party to the peace movement. Hubert Humphrey, the eventual Democratic Party nominee once Bobby Kennedy was assassinated, pushed McCarthy aside, and of course, went on to lose to Richard Nixon. Carter blazed his way from an unknown to the presidency during one of those times in American history where an opening existed for something new and essential to find its way into the political process. Yet the opening was lost to Ronald Reagan four years later.

Eugene McCarthy showed great courage in 1968 running against one of the most powerful presidents in our history. Lyndon Johnson eventually refused to run for a second term. By McCarthy stepping forward and finding the voice of so many disaffected in this country he may have blunted a more revolutionary solution. This could be seen as a good or a not so good thing depending on how radical your political persuasion was at the time. Certainly courage is not one of the characteristics lacking in one with a poetic voice.

My Lai Conversation[1]

How old are you, small Vietnamese boy?
Six fingers. Six years.
Why did you carry water to the wounded soldier,
now dead?

Your father.
Your father was enemy of free world.
You also now are enemy of free world.
Who told you to carry water to your father?
Your mother!
Your mother is also enemy of free world.
You go into ditch with your mother.
American politician has said,
"It is better to kill you as a boy in the elephant grass of Vietnam
Than to have to kill you as a man in the rye grass in the USA."
You understand.
It is easier to die
Where you know the names of the birds, the trees, and the grass
Than in a stranger country.
You will be number 128 in the body count for today.
High body count will make the Commander-in-Chief of free world
much encouraged.
Good-bye, small six-year-old Vietnamese boy, enemy of free world.

Jimmy Carter has been seen universally as an unsuccessful President and yet a very successful ex-President going on to win the Nobel Peace Prize for his humanitarian work around the world. He certainly opened the presidency to the empathy and compassion that are traits of those with poetic sensibilities. Still, he is seen by some to have been lacking in the kind of character traits that would allow him to navigate the hostile world of politics in this country.

Why We Get Cheaper Tires from Liberia[2]

The miles of rubber trees bend from the sea.
Each of the million acres cost a dime
nearly two Liberian lives ago.
Sweat, too,
has poured like sap from trees, almost free,
from men coerced to work by poverty
and leaders who had sold the people's fields.
The plantation kiln's pink bricks
made the homes of overseeing whites
a corporation's pride
Walls of the same polite bricks divide
the worker's tiny stalls
like cells in honeycombs;

no windows breach the walls,
no pipes or wires bring drink or light
to natives who can never claim this place as theirs
by digging in the ground.
No churches can be built,
no privy holes or even graves
dug in the rolling hills
for those milking Firestone's trees, who die
from mamba and mosquito bites.
I asked the owners why.
The cost of land, they said, was high.

Jimmy Carter, Always a Reckoning, 1995
(from the website ww.bong-town.com/Bong_Town/Liberia/
Poems/firestone.html)

Mostly poetry is left to galvanize the political process in the hinterlands, out where the people live and die. The link between poets and politics goes back almost to the beginning of time and certainly looms large in the period of the Vietnam War. Many poets through history saw politics as fit material for poetry. The political lives of a people color so problematically all areas of one's life. Walt Whitman wrote of Abraham Lincoln and the Civil War. Wilfred Owen wrote movingly of World War 1 and its cost.

The Parable of the Old Man and the Young[3]

So Abram rose, and clave the wood, and went,
And took the fire with him, and a knife.
And as they sojourned both of them together,
Isaac the first-born spake and said, My Father,
Behold the preparations, fire and iron,
But where the lamb for this burnt-offering?
Then Abram bound the youth with belts and strops,
And builded parapets and trenches there,
And stretched forth the knife to slay his son.
When lo! an angel called him out of heaven,
Saying, Lay not thy hand upon the lad,
Neither do anything to him. Behold,
A ram, caught in a thicket by its horns;

Offer the Ram of Pride instead of him.
But the old man would not so, but slew his son,
And half the seed of Europe, one by one.

(from the website
www.english.emory.edu/LostPoets/Parable.html)

Allan Ginsburg and Robert Bly, writing around the Vietnam War, are seminal voices in that period and much adieu is given them and many others for their part in energizing a culture to end that madness. And so poets engage seriously the political reality of their day.

Mao Zedong was also a poet and quite a good one it seems, as was Ho Chi Minh. Both of course serious revolutionary leaders.

Reascending CHINGKANGSHAN[4]

I have long aspired to reach for the clouds
And I again ascend Jinggang Mountain.
Coming from afar to view our old haunt,
I find new scenes replacing the old.
Everywhere orioles sing, swallows dart,
Streams babble
And the road mount skyward.
Once Huangyanggai is passed
No other perilous place calls for a glance.
Wind and thunder are stirring,
Flags and banners are flying
Wherever men live.
Thirty-eight years are fled
With a mere snap of the fingers.
We can clasp the moon in the Ninth Heaven
And seize turtles deep down in the Five Seas:
Nothing is hard in this world
If you dare to scale the heights.

Ho Chi Minh
Poems Written While In Prison[5]
Translated by Kenneth Rexroth

A COMRADES PAPER BLANKET

New books, old books,
the leaves all piled together.
A paper blanket
is better than no blanket.
You who sleep like princes,
sheltered from the cold,
Do you know how many men in prison
cannot sleep all night?

AUTUMN NIGHT

Before the gate, a guard
with a rifle on his shoulder.
In the sky, the moon flees
through clouds.
Swarming bed bugs,
like black army tanks in the night.
Squadrons of mosquitoes,
like waves of attacking places.
I think of my homeland.
I dream I can fly far away.
I dream I wonder trapped
in webs of sorrow.
A year has come to an end here.
What crime did I commit?
In tears I write
another prison poem.

CLEAR MORNING

The morning sun
shines over the prison wall,
And drives away the shadows
and miasma of hopelessness.
A life-giving breeze
blows across the earth.
A hundred imprisoned faces
smile once more.

So it is not that poets and poetry do not have a place in the political life of a people. And it cannot be said that poets don't know how to engage the political process whether from the presidency, the streets or from revolutionary necessity. So what is it that keeps the poetic sensibility mostly out of the political arena? The easy to blame scapegoat is the quickie sound bite, speedy image of pop culture, propaganda manipulated, fear induced culture of easy sounding solutions and then nothing really changes mentality. Here we visit the same old problems over and over and we blame the lack of real substantive change on the all embracing "terrorist" who now keeps us forever in their grasp and forever out of the kind of humane society we all desire. (Oh, where oh were has the red scare gone!) Rather it seems poetry forces the discussion to go to a level that so often is resisted in this culture.

Dan Brown, CBC News Online wrote on July 26, 2004 about "John Kerry's poetic gamble" in the 2004 election on www.cbc.ca/arts/features/poetryinpolitics.

"No matter which candidate wins this November's presidential vote, 2004 will go down in U.S. history as a remarkable election year. That's because John Kerry, the Democratic White House hopeful, has been reciting poetry as part of his stump speech. And that kind of thing doesn't happen often in America."

Poetry, as we know so dearly, demands some depth and it demands that the reader, listener likewise engage deeply. But how do we engage the populace in the deep discussion that is the purview of poetry?

Steve Kowit became a voice for Stand-up Poetry, a unique blend of the role of stand-up comic and the stage poet. Poetry and Jazz, first by Langston Hughes and then Kerouac and Ginsburg and now others brought the word together with jazz to energize the listener. The song lyrics of Leonard Cohen, Dylan, Paul Simon, Sting, and Bruce Springsteen push the poetic melody out on rhythm and harmony. Slams, rap, spoken word, hip-hop, the Internet all continue conveying the poetic line. Books still give us the tangible, in the hand feel and the chance to sit and deepen the experience. But mostly it seems it takes daring. Daring to find any means necessary to get the poetic voice out there in the face of the populace.

How Can Progressives Protect the "Atmosphere" of a Democratic Presidency

Jennifer Stone, long time commentator for KPFA—progressive radio—out of Berkeley, indicated in a show years ago that progressives were already critiquing John Kerry as not being far enough to the left. She called for a more even approach to Kerry's candidacy from those on the progressive left. This kind of critique of the Democrats is a staple of progressives whenever a Democrat finds their way to the White House. It is clear over the years that progressives have been critical in unseating and disarming both Republicans and Democrats that strayed to far from key elements of what is perceived as a humane, albeit, liberal agenda.

Progressives were instrumental in forcing LBJ to refuse the run for a second term. They were highly critical of Hubert Humphrey's failed run for president. With relentless pressure from progressives and others Agnew and then Nixon were driven out of office. Progressives were instrumental in creating the climate for Jimmy Carter to capture the White House. Though Reagan and then Bush senior keep the White House for 12 years, progressives kept the heat on and exposed amongst other improprieties their illegal contra war. Progressives launched Clinton into the Presidency, like it or not, and surely progressives created a climate to call Bush's arrogance into question and make a real space for Kerry to unseat Bush though this ultimately failed.

Progressive is a not so secret "code" word for all of those who seek enlightened change, from Democrats that are left of the center of that party, to liberals with socialist inclinations, to environmentalist, to peace activists, to out and out radicals that see the need for a major revolutionary overhaul of the American system. Central to the Progressive agenda is the critique of corporate capitalism (this may need to be redefined in light of Democatic Socialism) and US Military dominance in the world; the continuing hegemony of white male rule (the lack of multicultural inclusion and women's rights) both in US society and around the world; and the class based society that still dominates the US and leaves many on the lower socio-economic rungs out of the "American Dream,"—whatever that might be. Most on the progressive list believe in the American way of life and wish America to live up to its best principles and are deeply and incontrovertibly bound up in American institutions whether they be academic, professional, economic or religious, yet there are those considered progressive who wish for a different "experiment" in social order.

The desire for a social form that matches one's personal or group inclinations and values seems to be integral to what we understand as a fully developed person. One's social nature grows along with other more personal aspects of one's being and wishes for a full expression. Individual characteristics need a place to manifest and it can be catastrophic if this is not allowed to happen or is thwarted in some way. So too, it seems, that the part of one's nature that grows into a social being likewise wishes to have a means of expression out into the world—into, as it were, the social world. The fundamental principle of one's social nature, and the very foundation of social consciousness, is that it is inclusive, and not monolithic. The nature of healthy social behavior is that one may hold to one's beliefs and allow the beliefs of others to have a place in the larger community as well. What indeed would social mean other than the interaction with others? There may well be a part of the growing person that requires a monolithic nature, but in the social domain that is not the case.

Even in what appears to be monolithic cultures with dominant cultural forms we find there are various expressions as they move into the social realm. Within Islamic states there are Sunni and Shiite divisions. Within socialist ideologies there are the diversity of Marxists and Social Democrats, poles apart on many issues but still beholding to basic socialist views; even within Marxism we saw the Lenin/Trotsky/Stalin split plus many others. In the US there are the Democrats and Republicans, and other Parties, including Social Democrats. In our dear Republican Party, there are NeoCons and "Rockefeller" liberals (or there use to be). And of course Democrats are vastly more splintered than monolithic. In our present political environment, we are told that the polarization has reached an extreme not seen for sometime. This may or may not be the case. Not being a professional student of history still I recall that Jefferson and Hamilton lead significantly different factions of the new republic. Lincoln of course led the nation during its split into two states during the Civil War. During the run-up to the Second World War the country was split heavily and viable socialist parties were significant players on the political scene. The Socialist Party presidential candidate, Eugene V. Debs, opposed World War I; Norman Thomas ran for President in the Depression years of the 1930's.

At the time of my first presidential election Barry Goldwater and John Kennedy presented two very different views of the direction America would head. And of course, during the Vietnam era an opposition developed that over time not only helped bring that war to an end but also brought the country around to the realization that it was a war that should never have been waged.

So opposition is not a bad thing. In the realm of duality, that realm where everything is seen in its opposites, having competing views is the norm. Still, on occasion, we must find that place where we see through the duality and recognize the unity that is the foundation of all existence, including a country's. But, we must also recognize that there are times when we must enter the world of duality and resist one pole or another. Lord Krishna, in the Mahabarata, presents to Arjuna a great quandary. In the looming battle with Arjuna's family Krishna offers either himself as councilor to Arjuna or all of Krishna's cohorts, his thousands of warriors and confidants. Arjuna who is stunned that it should come to this eventually chooses Krishna; Krishna's cohorts go to the opposition and the battle ensues. Certainly this cannot be seen as a battle between good and evil as Krishna's cohorts are not also evil. There are many great lessons in the Mahabarta to be unfolded and at least one is that conflict is rarely between the ultimate good and the evil genius. Mostly it is between various views of the good but still it may be fought and so it is best that we recognize the humanity of all sides in the conflict and act accordingly.

But what does this mean to the progressive voice in our contemoray debates? A basic logical error one learns early in the study of philosophy is the ad hominen argument or the "argument against the man." When one fails to articulate the real flaws in an argument one proceeds to attack the individual who espouses that point of view. This sounds very much like the negative advertising that political contests eventual devolve into in this country. But this is very weak and assumes that we are addressing people who do not have the capacity to really understand what is going on. It devalues the individual and seeks to exploit the emotionality of the issue. Satirizing the foibles of a candidate may be legitimate, as on *The Daily Show*, but quickly turns into bad taste and character assassination when the focus is to demean. Progressives are guilty of this as well as archconservatives. But, as history will attest, even when this kind of behavior carries the day we can be sure that in the next go-round this kind of hostile behavior will be used, with greater rancor, on the candidate of our choice. This I believe is what Jennifer Stone was alluding to.

The extreme right abused Bill Clinton viciously during his Presidency, and yes he did bring some on himself. Did some of this stem from the viciousness of the attacks on Reagan and Bush senior by the left, possibly? Some of the ill will toward Clinton came from the more progressive elements on the left. I had a good friend who quickly withdrew support from Clinton soon after he became President because Clinton did not adhere to certain liberal agenda items that were dear to him. Did the right wing's attack on Clinton insure that Bush W would be treated in a similar way when he came into office, certainly and certainly Bush brought much on himself. What then will be the abuse heaped on a future Democratic Presidency?

Opposition at times must be total and still we must articulate what the "bottom line" truly is. Corporate business claims the "bottom line" to be its financial gain, political strategist claim the "bottom line" to be an all out win, no matter how. In both cases progressives must claim the "bottom line" to be that that holds the highest regard for human dignity.

Where does this lead? After 50 years of political awareness I firmly believe that progressive ideas and analysis have been the driving force for much that is good about America. From union organizing to the civil rights movement; from child labor laws to opposition to the death penalty; from women's rights to the peace movement, progressives have been out front analyzing the issues, forcing them before the American people, and demanding that politicians deal with them. The left of center agenda has held sway, but the more radical socialist agenda has not. That is a truth about American history and political life and must be dealt with. If progressives can continue to act in the name of the good and the true regardless of the outcome than a better American society is possible. This does not mean that ideals should be denied and it does not mean that dreams should be deferred. This does not mean that in the long term some very deep and fundamental principles of the "American experiment" don't need correcting. Democratic Socialism may indeed hold the form for a resurgence of a reevaluation of values in our social and economic life.

It is indeed possible to analysis American history to a point of denying its legitimacy; the original determination that a Negro was to be counted as but three-fifths of a white man, (no native americans/ no women) and even then only to give the south a larger population stake in the new congress, may well de-legitimizes the entire experiment as even once the change is made to full suffrage, still the social order is operating on this old primacy and yet now it is hidden in the political and social landscape (Jim Crow). Also the genocide of the native peoples give deep concern about the viability of this historical movement and raises again the question whether the words can be realized in the flesh. Still, ideals are important in moving a people towards the good and certainly figures like Thomas Jefferson can be seen in this light. And here we are more than two hundred year into it and gains have been made, corners turned and we must, it seems, continue on. It is the history of progressive gains that adds a new substance to the old history.

If progressives are to have a political role in a future Democratic Presidency, and we can hope, what should be the focus of the progressive agenda. Jerry Brown, in one of his runs for the Presidency, said something to the effect that, once one starts on the path to the Presidency one's choices become narrower and narrower. We see this in even the most liberal Presidents. It is against those historical conditions that drive most decision making that is a determining factor in much of what a President does. So, what is it that distinguishes a President like Jimmy Carter from a George W. Bush, a liberal from a conservative, a Democrat from a Republican? Given that many decisions will be mandated by the office itself, such as the threat of military force, used essentially by all presidents at one time or another, or the adherence to capitalist economic principles, the protection of trade, the appointment of essentially middle of the road politicos. What is the difference and why should progressives line up behind someone like a John Kerry (or a Joe Biden), a classic liberal (though his outspoken opposition to the Vietnam War gives him a special mandate in progressive circles)? That difference is "atmosphere." Yes, "atmosphere!"

Given that much of what a President can do is narrowly defined by the historical imperatives of this country still the nature of liberal philosophy gives the populous as a whole a greater opportunity to flourish and grow. Liberal philosophy and conservative philosophy differ in many respects but they different most essentially in their view of the individual. A conservative view sees the individual as essentially "bad" that is, needing strict outside control to insure right behavior, it is founded on a mostly Abrahamic view of original sin and the need for outside forces to bring the individual back to God or some state determined concept of the good. Like it or not, fascism is the outside extreme of a conservative agenda. The level of trust that individuals will behave properly is very low. Liberal philosophy is built off of humanistic assumptions about the essential good of the individual. Given the right conditions an individual will choose to do good rather than ill as it will lead to greater pleasure (and not the pleasure of gratification but the pleasure in living a good life). The classic liberal does indeed enjoy the good life (wine, cheese and a night at the concert) hand-in-hand with the good political battle. For the liberal, setting up the right conditions (atmosphere) is critical in creating the good society where individuals will do the right thing because it makes sense to do the right thing. Laws are still necessary but they can be less controlling of individual behavior and more controlling of what is construed as exploitive behavior i.e. wages lower than that needed to survive. Much personal behavior can be left in a non-legal status. Should there be laws about driving drunk, yes! should there be laws about smoking marijuana, no, this should be left in the non-legal realm.

And so the liberal "atmosphere" can assist in growing the progressive agenda but only if it is seen so, and only if it is utilized in a powerful way. What does an atmosphere mean? What might that be? Attitude, first of all! Atmosphere comes from attitude and attitude comes with that first essential view that distinguishes the liberal view from the conservative view. But, that is only the first, yet the necessary first condition. From that condition flows certain actions. LBJ's war on poverty flowed from that view, and his extension of the Vietnam War flowed from his conservative roots, he was a man and a President in deep conflict. This is not unusual in the American psyche. Jimmy Carter's liberal atmosphere flowed from a personal view of the good and he lived through that while his theology may well have thwarted some of what he could do. A man like Clinton had a better opportunity to express his liberal nature in his Presidency, and did so, and much of what he did accomplish was to create that "atmosphere" for the good to evolve. Much of his ability to act was stifled by the very conservative Congress and the extreme conservative forces that lined up against him. That is where the progressives must take aim in the eventuality of a future Democratic victory.

Progressives will hold the Democrat's feet to the fire on many issues, that is the nature of progressive action. But, to chip away at Democrats will be counter productive, what will need to be chipped away at is the extreme conservative forces that continue trying to permeate all aspects of American life. If progressive forces line up in a concerted way to take on those conservative element than that liberal "atmosphere" may allow some good to come forth. What must the progressive forces focus on?

First and foremost is to not give up mainstream media to the so-called conservative, anti-liberal agenda. Somehow in the post

Vietnam era conservatives were able to brand much mainstream media with a "liberal" bias (and continued under Trump) as if that were somehow bad and progressives could not and would not counter that tag and insist that if "liberal" media was infact the case than so be it. Infact progressives have gone on what could be considered a counter-offensive to paint the mainstream media as "conservative" and beholding to the large corporate conglomerates that own them. This, though beholding they are, is, I contend, counter-productive.

Failure from progressive forces to remember the past infringes on this "atmosphere". The issue of Vietnam military service brought up by Democrats during the Kerry/Bush Election was such an infringement. As a Vietnam Veteran and a veteran of the peace movement upon my discharge from the military, bringing up the issue of George W. Bush's military service lead to the bring up of Kerry's military service and his subsequent peace activities. To question Bush's service during a time when so many were looking for ways to protest the war and not serve in Vietnam was a foolish error on the part of the Democratic Party. I knew some who burned draft cards, some who fled to Canada, some who went to jail, some who used family deferments, some who stayed in school under less then sterling circumstances. Did George Bush use less than sterling mean to not go to Vietnam, maybe. Did Dick Chaney use less than sterling means to skip military service, maybe. Should these be reason for criticism, I say no, and to bring them up was a foolish political foible. To Kerry's credit he did not deny his peace activities and instead embraced them. The charge of not warranting one of his purple hearts was soon seen as grasping at straws (an ad hominen argument) on the part of right-wing critics.

Progressives need to be consistent and remember history. Vietnam War resisters need to be recognized as having placed their lives on the line to alter the destructive course that the country was on. Resisters need to be honored as heroes of the first rank in American history and given the recognition they deserve. No lines of demarcation should be made about the ways in which this resistance occurred.

River

The word river sounds like the river
But
not only does it sound like the whole
river that runs through Vietnam
through rice paddies and jungle and
villages because that's what language is
supposed to do
But it
sounds like the whole
river that runs through

Clearly progressives must take back the language that has been hijacked by an anti-intellectual right wing. Michael Moore in *Dude, Where's My Country?* began this process. In the chapter "A Liberal Paradise" he describes an extremely liberal country and ends by saying *"You don't have to go to the moon (to find this country) because...you're already there! This Land O'Left paradise I speak of is none other than...the United States of America!"* He is taking back the word liberal for all those in the US who infact share the values that the word stands for. It is now time to take back the term liberal from the phony use of it in the description of modern corporate capitalism or Liberal Capitalism as used in the current extension of corporate capitalism in the mostly non-white world. This capitalism has nothing to do with liberal and progressives must see to it that it is not attached to this extreme form of exploitation. To use liberal in this way confuses the understanding that many "average Americans" have regarding liberals. Are liberals part of that group of abusive capitalist? Also, to call this rewrite of colonialism globalization, or the global economy or world economy is a disgusting usurpation of the word global and world and all they stand for. When we talk about the world community or global community or global village we are not talking about the control of the world through corporate economic and political dominance.

Bopal

TV news report
of the Union Carbide pesticide leak, 1984
that poisoned and killed two thousand
in Bopal India.

This was immediately cut to a bombastic ad
for Vacation Holiday Cruises
to various parts of the world.

This image one on the other,
close to the new language of the earth,
so close to the earth in speech
that it cannot be misunderstood.

Close to one heart beating in another.

The same can be said about taking back the term and ideology of socialism. Bernie started this and progresssives must continue this effort.

As a poet who deeply understands that one of the functions of poetry is to take language back to its meaning and truth thorough the examined use of language, I also looks to a wider form of poetic discussion that through poetry insists that our social discussion seeks those truths in all discourse and expresses them fully. Progressives must be in the forefront of this and demand of the media the same. To challenge the right wing on these issues is paramount to protecting the "atmosphere" of a Democratic Presidency. If we allow the distortions of purposeful victories by conservative political "character assassination" on these sacred gains we are fools and worse.

Equating the liberation of women with the right to serve in combat and fly fighter jets is a usurpation of the women's liberation movement. Defining gay liberation by the recent push for gay marriage instead of for the right to be treated as an equal in society is a distortion of both the gay rights movement and the mostly progressive push in years past to break down the ridge barriers that

125

traditional marriage had built in the society including the shot-gun marriage, the dictums against interracial marriage, and the stigma against the practice of living together without being married. Progressives need to keep these issues out front. To applaud the black corporate CEO, while on Martin Luther King, Jr. Boulevard in Meridian Mississippi black people live in shacks that would have been a travesty in slave days, is a corruption of the "dream."

Yes, these are broad stroke issue and must be focused as they come up in each unique case but the issue here is where the progressive must focus their critique. If it become a critique of the Democrats policies and whether they are left enough we will have once again given the right the opportunity to sneak up and deliver blows that will dissipate the growing "atmosphere" of liberal/progressive possibilities. This would be another of the great mistakes that have plagued the left for so long, here and around the world. Do progressives have the discipline to extend the "atmosphere" into that world where we really will see a change of condition for those in need, here and abroad, I think so.

I Am a White Male

I published Leroy Moore's book "Black Kripple Delivers Poetry & Lyrics." a few years ago. Leroy really affected me. I like Leroy. He is the kind of person I wish to be inspired by, showing us how to include all people in our human community, encouraging all of us to give up our prejudice and ignorance. He works tirelessly for the rights of the alternately-abled, for the rights of blacks and women. May his love spread far and wide. Leroy has similar speech and physical patterns that characterize other "disabled" persons with whom he shares compassion. And, let me tell you, his intelligence far outshines mine and Trump's.

I can't even express how I felt when I saw Donald J. Trump's callous, disgusting, and abusive characterization of a disabled person.

Around the time of the Republican primaries, when it was becoming clear what kind of a man Trump was and the televised political "pundits" began to again spew out the stereotype of disaffected white men voting for the likes of him, I had a felt need to speak about an idea that first occurred to me forty years ago, in the blooming era of the "silent majority." Donald J. Trump is just the most recent candidate of a long line of politicians to employ the Southern Strategy.

Maybe today's voters have forgotten what that was. After the failure of Reconstruction in 1877, when Lincoln's Republican party withdrew the United States Army and federal support for the recontruction of Southern states, the Democratic party capitalized on post-Confederacy fears by intentionally instituting voting legislation that disenfranchised both blacks and poor whites: poll taxes, residency and literacy requirements. Jim Crow laws, "grandfather" voting clauses (a person could vote if illiterate, only if he had already voted prior to the Civil War), and the rise of the Ku Klux Klan solidified a racial caste system in the primarily Democratic Southern states for decades; until the Voting Rights Act of 1964.

Southern blacks regained the vote in an era when racial tensions were high; during an era when the populace was marching for the end of legal segregation. Generationally indoctrinated, disaffected

Southern white voters switched to the Republican Party so as not to vote "with" the black voters. Republican conservative presidential candidate Barry Goldwater swept the former Confederate states, but nowhere else in the nation.

Political strategists pounced, capitalizing on the desegregationist fears of that white demographic, with the false rhetoric of white superiority as a founding ethos of the country. By 1972, Nixon's "Southern strategy" was widely considered the path by which he won the presidency. Political strategist Lee Atwater mobilized the same demographic for Reagan. And then Atwater strategized with Roger Ailes (yes, the one from Fox News) for G.H.W. Bush. And here we are again.

Stereotypes of all sorts are false: mindless, ignorant and dangerous nonsense. If Americans don't look backwards, we are doomed to repeat an abhorrent history. May we extend to the masses a way to see through the false rhetoric so they may realize their interests are being manipulated and thrust back at them in a demeaning manner. By succumbing to media stereotypes, the Trump demographic are in fact placing America in great jeopardy. The fallacy of Manifest Destiny—that the white working male is the privileged "owner" of this country—perpetuates a divisive myth. Muslims and Mexicans are just the latest immigrants under threat. Chinese, Japanese, Italian, Irish; divide and conquer.

I am a white man (an older one), my three sons are white men, my two young grandsons are budding white men. I don't expect any of them to behave in such despicable ways, and I reject the implicit media stereotypes—racial castes are inherently wrong. Racial stereotyping began in the earliest iteration of this country as native peoples were marginalized in The Declaration of Independence. We must acknowledge that. The scurrilous denigration of women is also detrimental to our society. My daughter, the mothers of my children, my own mother and sisters and the myriad women who have blessed my life are being attacked. To whose benefit?

I have spent the last 50 years associating with people who have been working for civil rights, immigrant rights, workers' rights, LBGTQ rights, religious freedom and understanding, women's rights, and the freedom of people around the world not to live under the heel of economic and political subjugation. The opportunity to work with people who share these values—black, women, gay, Hispanic, Asian or yes, even white men—gives freedom (both intellectual and economic) to us all. So much is gained.

I want the media to find a more accurate and enlightened way to characterize the "older white men" demographic that supported, and supports, Trump rather than by employing the Southern Strategy and implying racial animus as the primary motive for their vote.

Act

I write as an act of revelation   that is it you know
So I can see what is there to be seen
Because so much comes our way

So many impressions   so much impinges on us
So many ideas and constructs   all of these bodies
In motion   moving before us   it can be hard to keep up-right
And so I keep a language available   ready to reveal what is there

It is not so hard to write   what is hard
Is to get the beauty down
Because that is what is at the center   that must be found

Stockton graffiti "Can I Live?" seen from Amtrak.

"This is what you shall do; Love the earth and sun and the animals, despise riches, give alms to everyone that asks, stand up for the stupid and crazy, devote your income and labor to others, hate tyrants, argue not concerning God, have patience and indulgence toward the people, take off your hat to nothing known or unknown or to any man or number of men, go freely with powerful uneducated persons and with the young and with the mothers of families, read these leaves in the open air every season of every year of your life, re-examine all you have been told at school or church or in any book, dismiss whatever insults your own soul, and your very flesh shall be a great poem and have the richest fluency not only in its words but in the silent lines of its lips and face and between the lashes of your eyes and in every motion and joint of your body."
—Walt Whitman
   preface to Leaves of Grass (1855)[6]

A Discussion of Poetics:
the Development of
Wholistic Forms of
Consciousness
and Poetry
Part IV

Synopsis of the
History of Consciousness

The interest in expanding consciousness occurs in all eras and shows up often in the art, poetry, dance, and music of the time, as well as the philosophical and literary writing of the day. It also is manifested in the lives of significant individuals. Certainly Plato was writing about expanding conscious awareness in *The Republic*. The "Allegory of the Cave," recognizes that we are not the constructs of our mind. Fyodor Dostoevsky moved into a powerful exploration of the deeply entangled mind in order to come to grips with his larger personal existence.

> It seemed clear to me that life and the world somehow depended upon me now. I may almost say that the world now seemed created for me alone: if I shot myself the world would cease to be at least for me. I say nothing of its being likely that nothing will exist for anyone when I am gone, and that as soon as my consciousness is extinguished the whole world will vanish too and become void like a phantom, as a mere appurtenance of my consciousness, for possibly all this world and all these people are only me myself. [1]

The poetry of Rimbaud, Baudelaire, Verlaine, and Mallarme' all engage us in a vast exploration of consciousness through the penetration of emotion.

Charles Baudelaire[2]
From Fuses I - on God
> Translated from the French by Norman Cameron

Even if God did not exist,
Religion would still be holy and divine.
God is the only being who, in order to rule,
Does not need even to exist.

The paintings of El Greco, coming when they did, clearly challenges the structure and perception of the day and lead, centuries later, to the paintings of Cezanne and Picasso and to the expanding view of reality that the Impressionists, Cubists, and Expressionists finally move towards.

> "The first painter who appears to have noticed the structural code in the morphology of the mature El Greco was Paul Cézanne, one of the forerunners of cubism." [3]

> "In any case, only the execution counts. From this point of view, it is correct to say that Cubism has a Spanish origin and that I invented Cubism. We must look for the Spanish influence in Cézanne. Things themselves necessitate it, the influence of El Greco, a Venetian painter, on him. But his structure is Cubist." [4]

The musical exploration of Bach, Mozart, Beethoven, Debussy, Ravel, Stravinsky are calling for us to grow into a wider more cosmic musical life. The dance of Isadora Duncan and Nijinsky manifest what the body can contain and express as consciousness. History is peppered with individuals who exemplify this expanded awareness in their personal existence: Lao Tzu, Gautama Buddha, Jesus Christ, Mary Magdalene, Gandhi, Saint Theresa of Avila, Walt Whitman, William Blake.

The modern interest in wholistic consciousness coming after World War II seems to be one of the first attempt to extend these experiences beyond the confines of the community of artists and special people and into the larger community. Though there certainly has been a roll back, this still goes on; young people are still on the quest. And yet other cultures may have integrated such a move many centuries ago. The Balinese people seem to have such an integration of the spiritual and aesthetic; the paleolithic cultures of old may have; the contemporary aboriginal cultures of Australia and the shamanic cultures of Latin American may have. Allen Ginsburg's reference to India in this regard is quite interesting. "Indians, really sophisticated as far as letting everybody be as crazy as they want and taking it as formal personal method of relating to Gods, all very proper and dignified." [5]

The question of the nature of consciousness and its significance to the culture's life has been much debated along with the method of attainment, particularly around the use of mind-altering drugs. But it seems clear that people will use a wide variety of methods in order to re-establish the link to a sense of unity that is at the basis of the quest for expanded consciousness; legislating what can and cannot be used has little impact on what in fact will be used. The benefit to a culture is exemplified in the reverence we show to those individuals who have embodied this sense of the unification of life. Also there is a curious tension between the experiential aspect and the presentational aspect. If the unitary nature of consciousness is likewise the central aspect of being, can that aspect of being be transmitted through art, poetry, music, dance, philosophy? If no, then what are their purposes; if yes, to what extent and to what end?

Lao Tzu was reluctant to write anything down, Christ and Buddha did not, yet we have their words. Poets and artists are reluctant to explain their work and music is peculiarly experiential in a way other arts must strive for. The experience of dance can really only be had by the dancer. Philosophy seems to be the furthest from the experience yet it may have the most impact on how cultures have organized themselves, for better or for worse; consider Plato, Aristotle, Confucius, Hegel, Marx, Locke and Jefferson.

Mind altering drugs have convinced artists at times that the product of art is superfluous because we cannot convey through any medium the true nature of the spiritual experience. Ginsburg went through such a period, unsure whether he should write poetry any longer. And yet poets are intrigued with "in the beginning was the word" as a recognition of the power of words, the voice, music, and sound as the generators of reality. Artists in general are particularly enthralled by the work itself, less so it can be said, by the profession of art. Through the writing of a poem, the painting of a picture, the production of music, the experience of higher consciousness is had; to this extent art of all sorts is closest to dance. The presentation of art

135

then has another function. It can be used to recall, to point a direction, to be a remainder and a catalyst for the experience, and at special moments to be a poignant link that generates the experience anew. Ginsburg's reaction to reading Blake; "I suddenly realized that this existence was it!" "This was the moment I was born for. This initiation, this consciousness of being alive unto myself. The spirit of the universe was what I was born to realize." [6] Blake was successful in transmitting his awareness.

I vividly remember, after spending time reading Dylan Thomas, his poetry, plays, biography, and being taken with his life and work, how he spoke to me, not as Blake spoke to Ginsburg—in a trance—but in the way I could create Dylan Thomas poetry, seemingly at will. Particularly while driving in the car, I could begin to speak out poetry that had the inflection, the language, the word play, and the images of Thomas' poetry. My voice would sound like his in that very personal, musical, rhythmic cadence that he spoke so recognizably. And I realized in this way the excitement of language, the beauty of words, the joy of creation, and the way in which ordinary life was imbibed with the magical qualities that we so often give only to the extraordinary because I would speak of things you might see while driving in a car. He spoke to me so well that his voice came through me in these moments of poetic outbursts. I've had to give this up for the most part in order to find my own voice, but it is still a wonder to me.

What all of these experiences of consciousness do is to let us know that we, as human creatures, are more than our provincial view of reality has lead us to believe. Carlos Castenada's explorations into a seeming parallel world of sorcery has, it seems, finally allowed us to accept the cosmology of native peoples on this continent, and recognize that their world, though different from Western-European based reality, is valid. We now explore with native people their shamanic relationship to nature and its powerful ecological understanding.

So what we have in all of these explorations is a growing awareness that may, if it does nothing else, give us the opportunity to live more harmoniously as people and as creatures on this planet because we have gained a glimpse of our place in the cosmos and, it is a far larger place than we previously imagined. It is a place that is connected to others in a far more intriguing way than our mundane life would have us believe. The unity that is the basis of consciousness gives us far more possibilities in the way in which we live and in the manner of our creations. We are open to the assemblage of artistic expression on a much vaster scale. We now have a better understanding of where all this created beauty comes from and why it is such an endless pursuit.

Introduction to the
Beat Literary Movement

The Beat Literary Movement, as exemplified by Jack Kerouac, Gary Synder, Michael McClure, Allen Ginsburg, Lawrence Ferlingetti, and others, embarks on a study of consciousness through their work. Its evolutionary history, beginning as early as 1944, has roots in many sources, particularly the tenets of Eastern spiritual thought, the spiritual poetry of Whitman and Blake, jazz—particularly bebop—the natural world, and the social struggles of the times.

During the 50s and 60s, and into the 70s, inquiries into consciousness were occurring in many disciplines. John Lilly was applying isolation experiments and computer theory with psychedelics and the study of dolphin language to form new ways of understanding human consciousness. Spiritual masters such as Oscar Ichazo were exploring various ancient spiritual disciplines using the methods of science to come up with models and forms for understanding and organizing consciousness in the contemporary world. Western trained academics like Timothy Leary, Richard Alpert, and others were experimenting with hallucinogenic agents. Claudio Naranjo, Charles Tart, Robert Orenstein, John White, and others, were advancing the inquiry.

There was a renewed interest in Eastern thought by some members of academia during this period, and an extraordinary surge in the development of new psychological tools. Ed Maupin, published the first study of the effects of Zen Meditation. Transcendental Meditation was vigorously studied in the late 60s because of the Beatles interest in the form, as was yoga and meditation which lead to the breakthroughs of biofeedback as a medical discipline. Much of this exciting growth in human understanding was going on against the backdrop of the popular use of, and popular exploration into, the mind altering qualities of various chemicals, as well as the scientific and academic inquiry into their effects, exemplified by Lilly, Leary, Alpert and others. Out of this inquiry and out of the renewed interest in such seminal works as Henry James' "Varieties of Religious Experiences," Aldous Huxley's "Perennial Philosophy," the body of Jungian psychology, and the unorthodox work of Wilhelm Reich, as well as the Buddhism of Alan Watts, a new understanding of consciousness as larger, more encompassing, and more exquisite than was thought possible was gaining entrance to a new generation of people.

For this book's application of wholistic forms of consciousness to poetics I chose the metaphor of human consciousness loosely based on the work of Oscar Ichazo called Trialectics and I look at how the Beat Literary Movement developed from the perspective of these new wholistic forms. I'll put forward, as well, an approach to poetics using the lens of Ichazo's work. The Beat Movement encapsulates during its history the elements that Ichazo describes in the development of the historical and psychic movement from formal, to dialectical, to trialectical (wholistic) forms of consciousness. I make no claim that these are the ideas of Ichazo only that they are an understanding that I came to as a result of some early work with Ichazo's spiritual systems.

Oscar Ichazo is a Chilean, trained in a wide range of spiritual forms from Buddhism to Sufism, new psychologies and martial arts. Ichazo sees occurring the next development of consciousness that is more in concert with a condition of unity.[7] Trialectics, (eco-logic) and other developments of wholistic thinking, arise out of necessity as tenets of formal (Aristotelian) thought, and dialectical (Hegelian) forms fail to account for our present world and fail in aiding us toward the solution of problems in our personal, social, and philosophical life. Trialectics is both a combining of formal and dialectical elements, and a further development of a wholistic, or a meta-logical view.[8] There has always been a prejudice against using logic, as we understand it, in looking at the arts. Ichazo and others have taken logic out of the confines of a linear perspective and recognize in trialectics a method of operating in a unified dimension; it brings in elements that historically have been dismissed in logic. John White in his introduction to the seminal 1972 volume "The Highest State of Consciousness" talks about enlightenment and the brain and says "the result is a new state of consciousness. This in turn creates a new mode of perception and feeling which leads to the discovery of non-rational (but not irrational) forms of logic, which are multi-level/integrated/simultaneous, not linear/sequential/either-or." [9] He is describing a wholistic logic found most often in poetry and the arts. The arts have always been the most unified presentation of reality.

Trialectics employs, in its basic method, four primary parts that can be applied to poetry and art in general: the attractive element, the active element, and a function leading to a result that moves from one manifestation to a more coherent place where one gains a more complete understanding and a more unified experience. Trialectics accounts for a growing change in conscious perception throughout the culture as exemplified by the Beat movement. The outline here is a very basic look at this approach as it applies to poetry and the arts in general and Beat poetry in particular. A more complete development of trialectics can be found in the writings of Ichazo, Horn, and others, referred to in the Appendix.

The remainder of this section unfolds in the following manner. The first section is a brief discussion of the Beat influences on consciousness and how consciousness has evolved over their history. Section two is a discussion of the four elements of Trialectics (eco-logic): attractive, active, function, and result, and a brief discussion of what eco-logic is about. More will be elaborated in the sections that follow. The third section is a look at poetry and its grounding in language, music, and the natural world. Section four looks at formal elements of poetry and their historical function and limitations. Section five will do the same for dialectical elements. Section six will elaborate on trialectics and its application as a poetic. Section seven draws all of this together with a discussion of poetic elements, the statement of a poetic, and the highest resolution of the Beat sensibility.

Beat Sensibility

The Beat poets offer in the body of their work a dramatic presentation of the movement from the collapsing formalist poetic world, (to which they were ardent contributors) to the chaos that welled up in their work as they experimented, through their lives, and documented through their work, the profound dialectical struggles of the post World War II period. The play of their work had, early in its perception, the transcending quality of Buddhism, which showed up in their developing poetic and social experience. Jack Kerouac wrote a sutra in 1956 at the urging of Gary Snyder called *The Scripture of the Golden Eternity.*

> 16
> The point is we're waiting, not how comfortable
> we are while waiting. Paleolithic man waited by
> caves for the realization of why he was there,
> and hunted; modern men wait in beautified
> homes and try to forget death and birth. We're
> waiting for the realization that this is the
> golden eternity.[10]

Buddhism provided the third impulse to a poetry that crossed to a new awakening consciousness. The first impulse, in the early years, was an intuitive recognition that the formalist elements, in the poetry of the day, needed to be overthrown. The second impulse was the prophetic insight that the social matrix was a death machine that would only succumb by a fierce head-on struggle.

The elements of conflict in the Beat's work and in their lives had the saving grace of the Buddhist transcendent quality of ordinary experience. They were constantly reaching for a frame of reference that left behind the tangle of the formal and dialectical world. Alan Watts, the Buddhist luminary amongst them, writes, "For the highest expression of Buddhism, both in life and art, is concerned with ordinary, everyday things, with birds, trees branches and wisps of grass, with gathering rice and drawing water." [11]

The development of the Beat poetic vision anticipated the social move to a new kind of consciousness. Ichazo likens the development of the previous forms of consciousness historically to the opening of new kinds of conscious perception in the psyche of the community where they arise. He says that with this view we can see that Europe functioned inside of the conscious tenets of formal, static logic, from the time of Aristotle until Hegel—and then Marx and Engels—realized that the problem of movement (particularly historical movement) needed a new logic, dialectical forms of thinking developed out of this. [12]

Consciousness in the west is changing and growing and the tenets of conflict, within a dialectical framework, do not account for the process that we see occurring, and the need we see arising; the need for cooperative forms of social interaction. Here develops new forms of consciousness, and new forms of conscious processes, closer to poetry and art.

The Beat movement anticipated and acted to facilitate this profound move to a new consciousness that was already awakening in the unconscious life of the people. William Burrough's wrote, "The Beat literature movement came at exactly the right time and said something millions of people of all nationalities all over the world were waiting to hear. You can't tell anybody anything he doesn't know already." [13] The Beats looked to Buddhism, and other Eastern spiritual disciplines, and found in them the form necessary to open, or relate, this new consciousness in the culture. A spiritual philosophy of process, the ordinary, and complementarity arose in the Eastern mind well before the Western.

The Beats brought this consciousness into the culture's life at a seminal time. Ichazo's work has acted to extend it in another way and give it a systematic form. It is interesting to note that what Ichazo sees as the historical move from formal to dialectical to trialectical consciousness was going on simultaneously in the Beat work. Almost, it could be said, a recapitulation of these conscious forces in a particular movement, all going on simultaneously, manifesting first as one, then as the other, all elements occurring at once, one long convoluted poem that encapsulates the process of consciousness going on in the whole society. The Beats then present it back to the society as the necessary reflection of the society's psychic life. Again from Burrough's, "There is no doubt that we're living in a freer america (conscious life) as a result of the Beat literary movement." [14]

Introduction to Trialectic

Trialectics is a method of looking at the nature of a process and, either recognizing significant elements that are at play in this process (the critical approach), or operating, as it were, inside these significant elements (a poetic).

Trialectics draws significantly from Taoism: the play of opposites (yin and yang) in dynamic balance; the recognition of the living quality of the world; and the recognition of the fundamental nature of change.

From Chapter Two of the Tao Te Ching

Therefore the sage goes about doing nothing, teaching no-talking.
The ten thousand things rise and fall without cease,
Creating, yet not possessing,
Working, yet not taking credit.
Work is done, then forgotten.
Therefore it lasts forever. [15]

China developed very early an understanding of the nature of process.

For this discussion a few distinctions between formal, dialectical and trialectical processes of thought need to be made.

This charting of Formal, Dialectical and Trialectical Axioms by Tomislav Budak from his 1995 essay TRIALECTICS - LOGIC FOR A NEW MILLENNIUM [16] gives a brief foundation.

FORMAL LOGIC AXIOMS

1. AXIOM OF IDENTITY $A = A$——the thing is equal to itself

2. AXIOM OF DISTINCTION $A \neq B$——the thing can be distinguished from things other than itself

3. AXIOM OF THE EXCLUDED MIDDLE $A \neq A + B$
——nothing is equal to both of two different things

DIALECTICS AXIOMS

*1. THE AXIOM OF QUANTITY AND QUALITY -
quantitative increase produces qualitative change*

*2. AXIOM OF INTERACTION OF OPPOSITES -
change results from the inevitable conflict
between opposing forces*

*3. AXIOM OF THE NEGATION OF THE NEGATION
- any thesis together with its antithesis (or
opposite) produces something different from the
two - a synthesis*

TRIALECTICS AXIOMS

*1.THERE IS A MUTATION FROM ONE MATERIAL
MANIFESTATION POINT TO ANOTHER
MATERIAL MANIFESTATION POINT (MMP)*

*a) The mutation is completed when inner
equilibrium has been achieved.*

b) MMP are neutral points of energy retention.

*c) The energy moves in a universe with
preestablished laws, preestablished MMP or within
preestablished models.*

*2. INSIDE OF EVERYTHING THERE IS THE SEED
OF ITS APPARENT OPPOSITE. THE EQUILIBRUIM
BETWEEN THE TWO OPPOSITIONS DEPENDS ON
THE BALANCED CIRCULATION OF ENERGY.
(attractive/active - my note)*

*a) From the point of view of nature, opposites do
not exist.*

*b) From the cosmic point of view, there are no
random accidents, but processes of circulation.*

c) In nature there are no accidents.

*3. THE PERPETUAL MOTION OF ALL CREATION IS
DUE TO THE INTERCHANGE OF ENERGY
BETWEEN MMP'S AND THERE IS, THEREFORE,
AN INHERENT ATTRACTION TO EITHER A
HIGHER OR LOWER MMP.*

*a) Higher MMP's are conformed by a smaller
number of factors and elements.*

b) Higher MMP's are responsive to the attraction of higher or lower correlating vibrations in a preestablished pattern.

c) One MMP's attraction to another can be ascending or descending.

A formal approach to consciousness, recognizes identity as a fundamental element. It allows for a fixed, static, identifiable world. In a formal world we can know what to expect. I am a writer, therefore I, and you, know what is to be expected. Between dialectical and trialectical thinking I'll use a single distinction. In dialectics the resolution of two elements (thesis and antithesis) occurs due to contradiction or conflict resolving into a synthesis (and thus creating a new thesis and antithesis). The process goes on and on. In trialectics these two elements, now called attractive and active, exist, but in a qualitatively different way, and the resolution between them is through complementarity or cooperation, giving rise to a higher or lower manifestation of the interaction. This distinction between dialectics and trialectic sets them clearly on different paths. Dialectics here is referred most closely to the Hegalian/Marxist dialectic in a social environment (though Ichazo has claimed it is the dialectic of Aristotle that he is concerned with). More can be said about these major elements in the history of philosophy as Budak has in his essay, yet this can be enough to move us toward an understanding as it applies to a poetic.

The first trialectical display in a process is the attractive, those elements that call the process into being. The recognition here is that things, events, behaviors, experiences, though arising out of nothing (the void) have an extensive complex of relevant material that brings them forth. This we recognize as the attractive force, it calls an involvement. If we look at a historical period like post WW II America many elements are presented: post-war militarism; the rise of industrial/corporate culture; the suppression of sexuality and art; black oppression; the growth of suburban boredom; grey flannel conformity. Along with this comes the stirring desire of bebop; rock's sexuality; youth restlessness; working class anxiety; the call of the road. The attractive wells up.

The active element is generally given credit for the doing, it is the element that is usually most visible. When we recognize the active element we have an opportunity to move in significant ways. We can now see the primary process. The active, if we look at the same period, can be seen in the saxophone of Charlie Parker, the fierce inventiveness of Miles Davis; the musical, male sexuality of Elvis; the new emerging sexual woman exemplified by Marilyn Monroe; Allen Ginsburg's "Howl"; Keroauc's "On the Road"; Bob Dylan's prophesies for a generation. Each of these creative acts actively gave voice to previously unexpressed, pressured feelings coming out of the yin field of post WW II America. These artists move trialectically to a higher resolution, while the mentality of McCarthyism, taking in the same field but in the worst and most antagonistic dialectical manner, attempts to maintain the old formal order and plummets to the lowest of the lows.

The function, as we will see in a later section, varies and gives us the means, the language, to either describe or engage what is now recognized as an on-going process. Function is important to the outcome both in the critical framework and in the framework of a poetic. Music, acting, poetry, and their disciplines are the function that brings the result into being.

The result is the last of the elements and is, in itself, only a particular point or complex brought out by the three elements (MMP). It is the moment of insight, the awakening in the process to its nature, the manifestation in tangible form (the poem or art), the Buddhist transcendent ordinary given conscious awareness. It is not created but revealed or recognized by the ensuing trialectical display. Marilyn Monroe in "Misfits" is the perfect revelation of the ordinary with the Buddhist quality of transcendence that raises the viewer to a clearer perception of Marilyn, her character, and the world she inhabits.

Poetry

Poetry by its nature is process sustained inside a set of words, language line, magical symbols, metaphors, rhythms. Justin Kaplan in his biography of Walt Whitman says, "Words, when he acquired language, became life itself, links to the external world and to his unconscious."... "A perfect writer (Whitman says) would make words sing, dance, kiss, do the male and female act, bear children, weep, bleed, rage, stab, steal, fire cannon, steer ships, sack cities, charge with cavalry or infantry, or do any thing that man or woman or the natural powers can do." [17]

Poetic writing attempts to allow process to continue inside of the poem's set of ultimately narrow parameters. As poetry develops, it presents/creates a felt experience, already of a unitary nature, and places it out into the world as rhythm, chants and song, and musical language. Whitman called his poetry "Songs." The weighting of music to word shifts from age to age and culture to culture: from tonal/musical languages like Vietnamese, where tonal elements convey and determine meaning, setting an emotional environment for the word, to lyrics presented with music as with the Minstrel of 12th Century Germany, or the troubadours of France, where the love-song's meaning rides on the musical line. [18] Primitive chants around an early fire give way to the repetition of a single sound or phrase imbibed with meaning and power in the meditative chants of Tibetan Buddhism and Hinduism.

At times words are associated strongly with a particular musical element such as the powerful rhythmic component of contemporary hip-hop, or the distinctive, melodic character of Gregorian Chants, where the music accentuates and is given preference over the words. [19] At other times music is used as background to words as in modern film and performance, where, at its best, as in "Laura's Theme" in *Dr. Zhivago* it infuses the film, and the dialogue, with strong poetic elements. At its worst music recedes and the words likewise lose form, think of much of contemporary action films and try to remember the music or dialogue.

Finally the balanced weighting of music and words is achieved in the single word, the purest language line, with music as an internal element, we call this poetry. Gary Synder says, "The real (poetic) line is in the music and the density...a musical density..." [20] Jazz, in its quintessential connection to a cultural feeling, reveals in itself a poetic nature one step before the word. With poets like Langston Hughes, jazz enervated the poetic line while the poet drew the meaning of the jazz experience into the poetic form. Jazz percolated into Beat consciousness and gave access to a language of formidable feeling. Jazz, the statement of black pain and dreams was one of the corridors that awakened white unconscious humanity. The Beats heard this and soon the music of jazz became an essential part of the Beat universe. Michael McClure speaks of finally hearing jazz in the music of Thelonnius Monk. "A very exotic, highly structured, mysterious, emotional occasion. Elegance. Elegance of the intellect and the body moving in tune with the elements. Because you have to, you have to move"... "I listened to the music for a year before touching it. Before it even got through my skin." [21]

Octavio Paz says, "languages are animated by something like a universal rhythm which is no different from that of music..." [22] Lew Welch writes, "You have a sense of language where language is held as music, where that music is the sound of a taut soul singing. You have this kind of sense of language for some mysterious reason. It is a mystery." [23]

Alfred Einstein in an "Essay on Music" titled *Words and Music*, though he comes from the beginning point of music, says, "abstract speech is unthinkable without rhythm and melodic flow." The "...intrinsic junction of word and tone show an ever-varying balance of these elements, that infact there is a continuous search for a different equilibrium, depending on the emotional or rational weight of a word." [24] He quotes Friedrich Gendalf writing about Goethe, speech itself "has a duel nature: it is both logical and magical." [25] Einstein says, "the elemental power of things sensuous is an innate quality of music," [26] and so also of poetry. J.W.N. Sullivan writes of Beethoven, that music is "...the mediator between intellect and sensuous life." [27] Music gives the poet access to the yin field, to draw out the nature of the experience in words. The language of poetry is drawn out of the sounds and textures of the sensuous, natural, musical, wild, mysterious world, a revelation of its process. From Welch, "Poetry is the sound of a man (/woman) in words." [28]

Language conveyed without internal music lacks this fundamental poetic element and constitutes one of the great debilitating errors of our age since it seems that the language of our mass culture is often devoid of music. Again Einstein, writing about the madrigal, "Music was elevated of the word, and for the word to be without music was almost as unthinkable as to be naked in the company of others. A conflict between words and tone, such as developed in later times, was impossible." [29] He may well have been thinking of our mass culture where music is everywhere, as commercial jingles, background to TV shows, pop culture, movies, etc., but in so many cases is little more than sonic diversion. Snyder, in talking about prose says, "prose does not have the musical phrase or the rhythm behind it. Nor does it have the content density or the complexity." [30] Mass language has music to an even lesser degree. Yet the matrix of our world is poetic. In fact, we recognize this by the use of the term "poetic" or "poetry," as in, the "horse galloped poetically" or descriptively in, "she was poetry in motion." When that elusive element is missing we are separated from the essential life of our world and we know it instinctively.

In order to see the application of trialectics as a basis for a "poetic" it is necessary to see how some formal elements and some dialectical elements have influenced poetry and how they have, at times, forwarded poetry and, at times, diverted it and, in a sense, impeded the natural poetic expression. I say impeded only in the large sense. These developments can be seen as in step with the times and hence functional to those times, even necessary, especially the dialectical element as seen in the Beat work. The elements of a trialectical approach can be seen as a way to realign with the poetic matrix of our world. The norm of great poetry has always been that it worked with the natural world and employed the elements that here are described as trialectical. Kaplan in reference to Whitman says, "only the completely healthy, integrated and functioning man, exercising all faculties and embracing all experience, was able to collaborate, as a peer, with nature." [31]

Formal Elements

When speaking of formal poetry we are usually referring to poetry that employs specific structural elements, these would generally be meter, rhyme, and strict form. In their historical use the elements of form gave the poet a means to build, out of the plethora of experience, an edifice, as it were, to reach the unitary experience. The structure of the poem fixed the experience, arresting at least a part of the process but leaving some as the poem held, through the form, the intent of the poet. Here lies, I believe, the notion of identity which Ichazo holds as critical to formal thought,[32] the building through structure a secure place from which to experience again what prompted the poem.

Here is a portion of a poem titled "Silence and Music" from Ursula Vaughn Williams, spouse of the composer Vaughn Williams, published in 1959. Clearly structured in a formal and regular manner including a rhymed pattern on line two and four of the stanza. It builds a structure to gain again the exquisite experience of the last line. It starts: "Silence come first:..." and the last stanza and line:

> "Voices of grief and from the heart of joy,
> so near to comprehension do we stand
> that wind and sea and all of winged delight
> lie in the octaves of man's voice and hand
> and music wakes from silence as from sleep." [33]

We are lifted to the sense of the last line on the structural edifice.

Louise Bogan, poet and critic, in an essay called *Formal Poetry* says, that the formal elements of poetry are meter and rhyme, but rhyme was not present in Greek and Roman poetry of the "great period" [34] and meter or rhythm is fundamental to all utterance and essential to all poetry. She leaves us with the sense that formal poetry is not a category that can be easily classified and neatly described either in its elements or in what those elements might have been that needed altering. So what is it that is indicative of its poetic limits? Bogan indicates that the exhaustion of traditional rhyme and structure was seen as the necessity for developing a new poetry not predicated on the classical model and not predicated on the iambic line, this occurs somewhere around the end of the 19th century beginning of the 20th century. Ezra Pound, T.S. Eliot, W.C. Williams, and others are given credit for this new impetus by the manipulation of the traditional iambic meter.[35] Whitman, coming earlier, was a lone voice. Whitman wrote, "Take no illustrations whatsoever from the ancients or classics..." [36]

So, in a sense, there is no exact corollary in poetry for formal Aristotelian processes. No specific defining characteristic. Rather, it seems, that the formalistic use of archaic forms and dated imagery, schooling formulas and stultifying teaching methods forced the break from old poetic ideals. James Karmen in his book on Robinson Jeffers presented him as the last of the classical poets although in many of his poems he transcended the formal approach. Karmen cites the formal approach as specific form, the grand declaration, and the reliance on Greek themes.[37]

Robert Bly in reference to Greek themes says of Gerald Nerval, who wrote in the mid 1800s, he "sensed that a genuine channel was about to open up between the European and the ancient Greek gods..." [38] Well, by the mid 1900s that channel had seriously collapsed, except in rare instances such as Rilke's Sonnets To Orpheus (more on this in the section on Trialectics). In Beat poetry there was a movement to the ordinary and away from the unfamiliar high born rhetoric of the classical metaphor. The Buddhist transcendent becomes full blown, the description of things in their magical ordinariness. Greek consciousness found its way into the deep psychological mythology and is still of great value in that dimension of exploration.

Jeffers becomes truly trialectical in many respects. Jeffers saw himself standing at the pinnacle of an age between the two world wars. "I believe we live about the summit of the wave of this age, and hence can see it more objectively, looking down toward the troughs on both sides." [39] The abyss maybe, but the poetry that comes after WW II, the direction the Beats took, was changed forever and Jeffers caught some glimpses. The opening lines from an early poem shows the learned fascination with the old poetic but the recognition of the impending change. From Prescription of Painful Ends:

> "Lucretius felt the change of the world in his time, the
>   great republic riding to the height
> Whence every road leads downward; Plato in his time
>   watched Athens
> Dance the down path. The future is a misted landscape,
>   no man sees clearly, but at cyclic turns" [40]

In a later piece called Vulture he shows this tremendous transcendence into a new age both of poetics and of poetry. Excerpt from Vulture:

> "I could see the naked red head between the great wings
> Bear downward staring. I said, "My dear bird, we are
>   wasting time here.
> These old bones will still work; they are not for you."
>   But how beautiful he looked, gliding down
> On those great sails; how beautiful he looked, veering
>   away in the sea-light over the precipice. I tell you
> solemnly
>
> That I was sorry to have disappointed him. To be eaten
>   by that beak and become part of him, to share those
>   wings and those eyes—
> What a sublime end of one's body, what an enskyment;
>   What a life after death." [41]

The Beat poet Lew Welch took up from this point in what I consider one of the most masterful pieces of poetry of any period. In Song of the Turkey Buzzard the poetic is contemporary; the intention of Jeffers is full blown and rides very high on the Buddhist idea of the awareness of all sentient beings.

Part II

Praises Gentle Tamalpais
Perfect in Wisdom and Beauty of the
sweetest water
and the soaring birds

great seas at the feet of thy cliffs

Hear my last Will & Testament:

> *Among my friends there shall always be*
> *one with proper instructions*
> *for my continuance.*

>> *Let no one grieve*
>> *I shall have used it all up*
>> *used up every bit of it.*

>> *What an extravagance!*
>> *What a relief!*

> *On a marked rock, following his orders,*
> *place my meat.*

>> *All care must be taken not to*
>> *frighten the natives of this*
>> *barbarous land, who*
>> *will not let us die, even,*
>> *as we wish.*

> *With proper ceremony disembowel what I*
> *no longer need, that it might more quickly*
> *rot and tempt*

my new form

NOT THE BRONZE CASKET BUT THE BRAZEN WING

SOARING FOREVER ABOVE THEE O PERFECT

O SWEETEST WATER O GLORIOUS

WHEELING

BIRD [42]

154

A poem done with an excess of form arrests the process that is central to poetry, usually through the excessive dominance of form over content. The content is made to fit the formal elements. Formal elements when used in a masterly way can sustain the process but when used with decreasing skill or as a requirement, become stultifying and the natural movement of the poem becomes rigidified. Formal elements can stop the process, giving it identity and a fixed place so that navigation through it can be known and anticipated. Poetry that relies on formal elements to an excessive degree not only fixes the content but identifies the voice as that of the author through the adept handling of formal elements rather than the voice of the experience. It also fixes the place and the method and creates an orthodoxy that determines future work. Post World War II academic poetry left poetry in a position out of which little of the "poetry of the world" could enter. It became an orthodoxy and hence becomes a block to creative movement.

Dialectical Elements

Dialectical poetry recognizes the dynamic movement always taking place. It recognizes the play of opposites, thesis/antithesis (the yin/yang, the active/attractive) although in contradiction. Dialectical poetry recognizes the place of the "I" in the content of the work or the content that is in critique. The "I" in this sense sets one apart from the process. It works both as a device of the poet, "I" the poet, and as a device that brings the reader to identify with the "I" in the poem. The recitation of "I" becomes the "I" who is reading, effective dialectically and certainly not exclusive to dialectical poetry. It can be a bridge that brings the reader into the poetic experience.

Dialectical poetry recognizes that the world is not fixed (though formal thought may wish us to believe that it is) and it drives for the underlying process that poetry seeks to present, but dialectics comes up short because it ultimately stands outside the poetic experience. It is a vehicle for beating against the confines of an orthodoxy. Its contribution has been greatest in exploding the myth of the formal world, opening it up again to movement and new ideas. In poetry it has been used most effectively in two areas: first in breaking out of the formal orthodoxy of traditional poetry and the imposition of that orthodoxy on emerging poets; second as a tool for breaking out of the political rigidity of the culture. The best example of dialectical poetry is the west coast poetry of the 30s, and early Beat poetry, that had as its objective the breaking out of the confines of the east coast hierarchy, and as a critic of pre and post WW II society. The Beats were "sweeping in their condemnation of their country's social, sexual, political, and religious values." [43] Kenneth Rexroth writes in 1970 of this time. "We finally broke it," east coast, British domination of poetry. "Nobody else broke it. We broke it. And we had damn few outlets." [44]

The critique of society was long and arduous and came in a sort of growing organic awareness. A short excerpt from a long poem by Lawrence Ferlinghetti titled, appropriately:

Autobiography

"*I have read the Reader's Digest
from cover to cover
and noted the close identification
of the United States and the Promised Land
where every coin is marked
In God We Trust
but the dollar bills do not have it
being gods unto themselves.
I read the Want Ads daily
looking for a stone a leaf
an unfound door.
I hear America singing
in the Yellow Pages.
One could never tell
the soul has its rages.
I read the papers every day
and hear humanity amiss
in the sad plethora of print.
I see where Walden Pond has been drained
to make an amusement park.*

156

I see they're making Melville
eat his whale.
I see another war is coming
but I won't be there to fight it." [45]

Dialectical poetry when handled poorly (Ferlinghetti handles it well) becomes little more than sloganeering and the active element becomes overbearing and strident. Pablo Neruda was probably the best practitioner of dialectical poetry both from the political stand and in the use of poetic elements. Neruda worked tirelessly at giving voice to all elements of his world and he gave no less attention to the political. As a Marxist much of his adult life he gave voice to the errors of his time, the need for change, and the play of opposites that had come to such a critical level throughout the mid 20th century. [46] His poetry was passion and power in its dialectical playing out.

The Steel Gathers (1945)

I have seen evil and evil men, but not in their
        lairs.

Evil in a cavern is a fairy tale.

After the poor had fallen
into tatters, into the wretched mine,
they filled their road with spooks.
I found evil seated in the courtrooms:
in the Senate I found it dressed
and groomed, twisting debates
and ideas toward its pockets.

                Evil and evil men
had just taken a bath: they were
bound in satisfactions,
and were perfect in the smoothness
of their false decorum.
                I've seen evil, and to
banish this pustule I've lived

with other men, adding lives,
becoming a secret cipher, nameless,
invincible unity of people and dust.

The proud man was fighting
fiercely in his ivory closet
and evil flashed by
saying: "His solitary
rectitude is admirable.
Let him be.

The impetuous man unsheathed his alphabet
and mounted on his sword he stopped
to perorate in the deserted street.
Passing by, the evil man told him: "How brave!"
and went to the Club to comment on the deed.

But when I was stone and mortar,
tower and steel, associated syllable:
when I joined hands with my people
and went to combat with the entire sea:
when I abandoned my solitude and put
my pride in the museum, my vanity in the
attic with broken-down carriages,
when I became party with other men, when
the metal of purity was organized,
then evil came and said: "Hit
them hard, let them rot in jail!"

But now it was too late, and the movement
of man, my party,
is the invincible springtime, hard
beneath the earth, when it was hope
and common fruit for the future." [47]

And he of course navigated far beyond this realm. From the
book Stones:

                    IV
"When everything was high,
height,
height,
the emerald cold waited there,

158

> *the emerald stare:*
> *it was an eye:*
> *it watched*
> *and was the center of the sky,*
> *center of empty space:*
> *the emerald*
> *watched;*
> *unique, hard, immensely green*
> *as if it were an eye*
> *of the ocean,*
> *fixed stare of water,*
> *drop of God,*
> *victory of the cold*
> *green tower."* [48]

Formal thinking results in mathematical logic and the extreme form of machine logic devoid of the essentially human. The so-called information age is its natural progression. A proliferation of things laid out in a linear manner that never resolves into anything. At best we have a multitude of structures to build off of. The computer and its many programs have value only in what they can be coaxed to do. Dialectical thinking reaches a point where it devours itself. Marxism shows this extreme where before the transition to communism—which requires a new wholistic logic—the socialist state succumbs to its own antithesis and is dissolved. Communism in our modern era must either find this new form of consciousness or it will not live through its present crisis. So too in dialectical poetry. The formal poetic resolves into nothing and into its inevitable, WW I, WW II, WWIII (eco-disaster) to come. Dialectical poetry rails on eventually becoming a parody of itself, a dissolving of its own importance, difficult to listen to as well as dated and lacking in universality.

Trialectic Elements

In a poem seen trialectically the general tendency will be to see the development of the attractive (yin) element first, allowing the active (yang) to emerge. Less emphasis is placed on predetermined content; content will be the expanded field. Content will be an emerging phenomena and will appear quite large and mostly unstructured, at least at first. Almost nebulous, it will act attractively, magnetically, a tugging or pulling towards the elements that requires delineation. Snyder says, "The inner world is too large to ever put down; it's a sea, it's an ocean."[49] This is the yin field. The Tao Te Ching presents the most elusive yet rich description of the all pervasive yin field.

Six

The valley spirit never dies;
It is the woman primal mother
Her gate way is the root of heaven and earth.
It is like a veil barely seen.
Use it; it will never fail. [50]

And from One.

Darkness within darkness
the gate to all mystery. [51]

The voice will emerge from this field and carry the active/yang toward a re-balancing into a region of greater resolution. It will act as a clarifying medium that strongly wishes to resolve what the yin field has presented but it will take a far reaching course and present the yin field, drawing conclusions if that is what is needed; being descriptive if that is what is called; being a change agent if that is to be done. Its voice must be in concert with the yin field. Lew Welch talks about voice in terms of the tribe, "...what their tribe is speaking"..."it can be used by the tribe in moments of need."[52]

The active is seen as the seed of the attractive as the attractive is the ground of the active. The active is the voice inside of the attractive field, it lies waiting to be called out.[53]

We find in the development of bebop the difficult course the yang/active voice had to take to break through the structure and confinement of the formal world gone crazy in WW II. The struggle within the music to overcome the contradictions of the dialectical movement of history as the black race calls out into the void of consciousness for liberation from the physical chains of slavery's historical remains and from the continuing psychic bondage of the spirit. Charlie Parker in music and life shows the great power of a true active principle responding to the attractive dream of black people's longing, through the cultural field of jazz. Listen to Parker's masterful expression (*Ornithology, Anthopology, Scrapple from the Apple*). The result is a new jazz expression that is itself part of the new attractive field.

Rainer Maria Rilke, writing about how the *Sonnets to Orpheus* came about, says, they were *"perhaps the most mysterious... in the way they came up and entrusted themselves to me, the most enigmatic diction I have ever held through and achieved..." "How should one not increase in reverence and infinite gratitude over such experiences in one's own existence?"* [54] The attractive called his active poetic voice, the poetry came full born. His poetic voice was the voice of the work, the Greek metaphor was open. Sonnet Number 5 of the First Part of:

Sonnets To Orpheus

> *Set up no stone to his memory.*
> *Just let the rose bloom each year for his sake.*
> *For it is Orpheus. His metamorphosis*
> *in this one and this. We should not trouble*
>
> *about other names. Once and for all*
> *it's Orpheus when there's singing. He comes and goes.*
> *It is not much already if at times*
> *he overstays for a few days the bowl of roses?*
>
> *O how he has to vanish, for you to grasp it!*
> *Though he himself takes fright at vanishing.*
> *Even while his word transcends the being there,*
> *he's there already where you do not follow.*
> *The lyre's lattice does not snare his hands.*
> *And he obeys, while yet he oversteps.* [55]

Function most often will show up in the form, where structure and language will change and vary in order to get at the yin/attractive field. The development of a discipline and the various methods of study needed to convey are at the heart of function. Voice will utilize function reaching for a higher resolution. The over-all effect will be toward re-balancing at a new and more stable condition that will allow a higher level of maintenance. Ichazo calls this a material manifestation point and states that these are pre-established laws or patterns.[56] Buddhism would recognize them as natural places. We move to them because they are points of fundamental cohesion of a higher or lower sort. The form brings the conditions together for these manifestations to emerge.[57] We are not creating something that does not exist, it exists and the voice will reveal it.

The trialectical method appears weaker and less determined and more overall feminine and yet it leads to the stronger, more stable structure. It is also open to more elements impacting it and hence it appears to make specific goal directed behavior more difficult. This appears so except when the goal is seen as operating within unity, which is in fact Ichazo's stated purpose. Unity is not here used as a generic term but unity as a spiritual condition. Great music and poetry show the intrinsic unitary and universal nature of this form of consciousness.

Trialectics can then be seen as a method that applies when unity is achieved and not to gain unity. This distinguishes it from a formal approach which builds toward a unified experience. Trialectics is the process of the unified condition. This distinguishes it from a dialectical approach which seeks unity in conflict and fails. Trialectics is the method of movement inside the field of unity, the field of reality, wilderness, music, or the poetic matrix. It is another way of recognizing the Buddha nature or universal consciousness. Logic loses its dictum as a form of exclusion, linear and confining, and is seen as the way consciousness moves with the field of unity, in preparation for letting go of the method as well.

Poetic Elements

Trialectic elements; attractive, active, function, and result, relate to some of the major elements of poetry and all art. Starting with three major artistic elements; form, content, and voice, form will mostly be the function, as we have seen in previous discussions. The form is the carrier, that which gives shape and direction. It sustains the other elements and the potential of movement from one state to another that is a central purpose of trialectics. It is the discipline between the yin and the yang, the vehicle to speak and present. Form can be seen most revealingly in stages of breakdown where energy is loosened in preparation for a recombing into a higher or more resolute form, or when form is handled poorly and becomes obvious. Form is most readily seen as structural elements. For the poet, language, words, line, rhythm, repetition, metaphor, etc.

Content can most often be seen as the attractive element. Here is where the poem sets the ground, the element that gives substance and defines the intention, purpose and direction of the work. It can be the descriptive element, setting, scene, time and place, as well as sensory and intellectual elements. It can be broadly philosophical or as simple as everyday events or natural phenomena. Content is context and reason in the broadest sense out of which is drawn what the poem will be. In reference to Basho, his disciple Doho says, he would "enter into the object, the whole of its delicate life, feeling as it feels. The poem follows of itself." [58]

It starts large, everything within the field, all information, all experience and perception, all possibilities. It is vast and expansive but it is not without boundaries nor is it without purpose. The transition into poetry will define the boundaries, and what is needed will call the voice. Those elements called "beat" in the early descriptions of the movement, "exhaustion, at the bottom of the world, looking up or out, sleepless, wide-eyed, perceptive, rejected by society, on your own, streetwise;" Kerouac's insistence that the "object of the quest was spiritual;" [59] Rexroth's characterization of "Howl" as "The confession of faith of a new generation;" [60] nature and the ecological, all this was the content, the attractive, the yin field. A new revelation of reality, the poetic matrix, wilderness, has been uncovered and is visible in the world, new in its manifestation as art, new in its expression of unity.

Finally, voice. Voice here refers not to the poets voice but the voice of the work or the experience. Poetry, unlike many other forms of art is most often taken directly from the poets speaking, where fiction will often be from the vantage point of a character, and so it might be easy to mis-identify voice in poetry as that of the poet. But voice here is seen as the active element that is brought forth from the content, the yin field, itself. It might be the voice of an identifiable group such as the black voice that permeates jazz and lyrics of rap; or it may be the voice of universal experience that comes through in much spiritual work, or that of the "god experience" that is true of Rumi. Feminist poetry speaks with the woman's voice, Snyder as the voice of nature, or Whitman as the voice of a country. And so voice is that emergent active element around which coalesces the movement drawn out of the content or attractive source and carried by the function element of form. The result is a greater, more unified condition where a new equilibrium is achieved, balance is restored and structure assembled to support the new condition.

Intention is part of the active element. You move carrying an intention into the undifferentiated attractive world, joining with that world by study, by experience, by knowing the names of things, the interactions, the origins. By eating it, making love to it, sleeping with it, listening and conversing until you are able to coalesce with what is significant, what is to be done, or known or revealed. The attractive element is the element that reveals and then sets the task or action to follow.

But it is the intention that seeks out the call or as Snyder says, "disciplined inattention." [61] It is the active element. It is held up as a question or place of consequence. It can't be too specific. It is not a demand or a decision that such and so is to be.

The active element finally must move with patience, with calmness and with a gentleness that recognizes that much of what can be revealed is very subtle and depends on a quietness and simple resolve.

The yin store is vast and complex, full of a miracle of particulars all connected and interrelated. It will reveal itself whether asked to or not. Its revelations are continuous and unstoppable. The yang makes choices, filters and draws parameters in certain directions and asks certain questions and then waits for the yin to present what is there.

Both attractive and active can learn a language, or a discipline with which to communicate. This function then lies between them and acts as a refining medium to present the material gathered.

M.C. Richards in her classic *Centering - In Pottery, Poetry and the Person* says, "Ideas do not belong to people. Ideas live in the world as we do. We discover certain ideas at certain times. Someone enjoys a certain revelation and passes it around. A certain person's courage inspires courage in others. People share their culture: there are enjoyable resemblances that make us feel like a community of fellow beings, fellow craftsmen—using a tradition and contributing our own impulses to it." [62] Here she recognizes the attractive, the active, the function and the result as evoking the highest that a culture of people can find. She recognizes the process that is the natural condition of humanity.

A poem from a trialectic perspective would, through its process, recapitulate the unitary experience. Where, in formal poetry, the form might stand out, here the form would be invisible, an element hidden in the process of accomplishment. The dialectical play of opposites would dissolve into attractive and active realizing what is to be presented.

Significantly, poetry can be read as individual pieces and each piece, line, image, would contain the full, whole experience; or a manuscript can be read from start to finish, the whole manuscript a unity and each piece a facet in the holography that is the work. McClure speaks in terms of the body, it is a "beatific complex meat structure that you are a tentacle, an aura, an extrusion, an experiencing of," the work comes out of this. "The body of the universe manifested in our body." [63]

Throughout is a refining and a polishing that can ultimately lead to art. This is where the attractive gives and the active intention gets set down as elements that bring into view and present to the world. When this is achieved, a higher level of manifestation is brought into being; here is a point of clarity, a condition of reality that though simple in view creates a wider and more plausible condition to exist. Its stability is greater without being confining and it allows for moments of insight, places of rest and sustenance, and moments of peace.

The Woodcarver from Chuang Tzu is, in its form, an exquisite example of a trialectic poem, and not only in form but in content it gives one of the most lucid presentations of the elusive process itself. To combine this into one work is one of the most wonderful accomplishments that I have seen in all poetry, all art.

The Woodcarver

Khing, the master carver, made a bell stand
Of precious wood. When it was finished,
All who saw it were astounded. They said it must be
The work of spirits.
The Prince of Lu said to the master carver:
"What is your secret?"

Khing replied: "I am only a workman:
I have no secret. There is only this:
When I began to think about the work you commanded
I guarded my spirit, did not expend it
On trifles, that were not to the point,
I fasted in order to set
My heart at rest
After three days fasting,
I had forgotten gain and success.
After five days
I had forgotten praise or criticism.
After seven days
I had forgotten my body
With all its limbs.

"By this time all thought of your Highness
And of the court had faded away.
All that might distract me from the work
Had vanished.
I was collected in the single thought
Of the bell stand.

"Then I went to the forest
To see the trees in their own natural state.
When the right tree appeared before my eyes,
The bell stand also appeared in it, clearly, beyond doubt.
All I had to do was to put forth my hand
and begin.

"If I had not met this particular tree
There would have been
No bell stand at all.

"What happened?
My own collected thought
Encountered the hidden potential in the wood;
From this live encounter came the work
Which you ascribe to the spirits." [64]

A fully mature example of a trialectical poem in form, content, and voice is Gary Snyder's *Three Deer One Coyote Running in the Snow*. The elements are masterfully at play. The attractive is the vastness of the wild as evident by the interaction of deer and coyote, snow and poet. The active is simple, a mere observation of the interaction, the willingness to be an agent for writing it down. The function, the structure, is transparent, simple lines with holes and spaces to let the image come through. The result is a seemingly simple event that occurs often in the natural world, but, in the last line, we are elevated to a sense of the transcendent ordinary. It is a simple event but in the willingness to be a part of it, all of the complexity of the wild is spread out before us and the "I" which was Snyder is now us.

Three Deer One Coyote Running in the Snow

        First three deer bounding
and then coyote streaks right after
        tail   flat out

I stand dumb a while   two seconds
blankly black-and-white of trees and snow

        Coyote's back!
        good coat, fluffy tail,

sees me: quickly gone.

        Later:
I walk through where they ran

        to study how that news all got put down. [65]

Meditation
Part V

Introduction

In all preceding sections, and in the section that follows, central in this undertaking is the place of meditation in gaining a depth of understanding needed to follow what becomes a natural progression. Meditation, introduced in earlier sections, is articulated here as best as can be done for a subject that is clearly outside of the ability to do so. As has been the case in all preceding sections this presentation is used to come up close to the subject with at least some understanding of what is going on.

Alan Watts in one of his early writing, *How Buddhism Came to Life*, 1939, says of Mahayana Buddhism:

"Thus, whereas ordinary men think there is a difference between themselves and the Buddhas, the Buddhas see no difference and hence have no spiritual pride. But the understanding of their identity with the ultimate reality of the universe gives them the use of a creative freedom and power of spirit which ordinary man has but does not appreciate."

Here then is a very succinct statement of what it is that meditation is about. Simply put, it is the vehicle for recognizing our identity with the ultimate reality of the universe and that this unity is already the case for all beings, ordinary or Buddhas.

Centering

Go to center without expectation,
enjoy the expression that comes.
Buddha shows us that center is silence and the rose,
and the perfect poem nothing at all.

And so the poem uses only enough words
or sounds to hint at silence and convey it.
Meaning would be but a chimera.

Each time center is lost and noise consumes,
return to center, to nothing,
sit quietly and accept everything.
In the city noise is everywhere
and wants us to make poems of noise.

Center is best found in wilderness;
and in the city must be found within.
In seeking it is good not to forget that center may be found out
there, amidst cars and sirens, street lights and traffic signals,
but it is hard.

Return to center, find a quiet place
that is easier found in the far off desert
or the high exotic mountains
where sounds are breath.

Utter a few chosen words that give body to silence
extend them into the world,
to be looked at, touched, felt, passed along
and not captured at all.

Where We Start

We have, because of the need to distinguish ourselves—primarily in the social world—become identified with a part of ourselves that is a necessary and exquisitely valuable aspect of our being. Ego strength or ego consciousness arises in many complex ways. On the one hand it can be seen as a very positive part of the complex that is our personality that becomes self-enhancing as a means of moving through the social world. A strong well constructed ego, that operates on sound principles for the good of the individual and the community has great value. It is most significant when it is recognized as merely a construct, an aspect of the boundariless whole and ultimately without permanence. All spiritual forms teach that we dissolve from this condition and die into god, rejoining the undifferentiated mass out of which we came.

On the other hand because life is filled with trauma, because the good rides hand-in-hand with the bad, because power sits at one time with those who use it wisely and well and at other times it sits with those who are either foolish or sinister, ego often develops a destructive, dysfunctional element. It goes so far as to become the primary negative descriptor of a culture; in its often marginal and dangerous form as the nature of a group. Nazi Germany's racial superiority is the classic example.

When the negatively developed ego becomes dominate in a person or a culture, we feel cut off, isolated, constricted, and fearful and even dangerously destructive. An over-arching sense of personal self arises but it sits on a powder keg of emotion because it has become walled in by the ever narrowing sense that only "I" exist and all else is threatening. When this manifests in a person, real danger to oneself and to others can occur. When it arises in a nation or culture, internal strife becomes the norm because all or most members take on that form, war between nations becomes very likely. When this negative ego is less severe the individual or the group, though they may not manifest outwardly destructive behavior, lives in the interior with pain, dysfunction, and a personal or cultural sense of disintegration and chaos. The period of the Vietnam War and its after math manifested both of these conditions remarkably on a cultural level.

Where then does meditation come in? Usually at the moment when a person or culture reaches the point of greatest isolation and pain, if they are fortunate and have maintained at least some awareness of their greater connection, they begin a journey seeking a way out of the pain, beginning a move towards that greater connection. They may seek through meditation a way to do this. From a cultural stand point this movement must come as a result of the desire of its members.

Meditation, or the recognition that we come to a sense of our greater connection by doing nothing, finding again the silence that is our center, becomes an on-going discipline, frustrating at first because the personal and social ego structure impinges on us relentlessly. It is a discipline that we come to again and again.

Self-observation is the first tool of meditation that brings us into unity with universal reality. Self-observation turns eventually into mindfulness as meditation deepen. But self-observation or the willingness to watch the processes of our mind/body is the beginning point in the unfolding of the meditative life.

After initial frustration in our attempts at self-observation we gain one of the first over-arching lessons about life and that is acceptance. As we sit in meditation and watch, feel, experience the chaos of our mind, body, emotions, life experience, the dysfunction of our cultural forms, the absurdity of our prejudices, we finally accept that this is in fact the case and it will, to a lesser or greater degree, continue to be so. At each moment the whole manifests and through acceptance we are connected to the reality of the universe, we recognize our place in it and the continuing drama that is our life. Now, through relaxation, breathing, self-observation, and acceptance we can begin, through meditation, to enhance that greater connection.

The next step in meditation, once the acceptance has become real and we see the almost relentless chaos of our life—our mind—is the process of letting-go. This letting-go can sound like so much jargon but it truly is a letting-go.

In Meditation we are taught to observe the content of our thoughts without judgment, to see them pass as a stream through our mind and to let them go recognizing that they are us and not us. If we

174

find that we follow them like chasing rabbits down myriad rabbit holes we let them go and return to self-observation. Letting-go applies in our emotional life as well. Letting-go of our past, our karmic ties, our negativity, our dependency, and often even our physical possessions. Letting-go is not the sum of this particular phase but it is a vehicle for lessening what is not essential so that room is made for something of infinitely greater value. Letting-go is the vehicle for making room for that which we did not know was available to us because of the accumulation of our past and the attachment through emotion or belief that we maintain.

A resting point in the meditative process comes when we begin to see the world as it is. It is not a place of great elation, nor a place of significant change in one's life. It is part of the awakening and as the awakening continues it can be a burden, a sadness, a pessimism where we say, "this is all, just this?" Peggy Lee, the beautiful Jazz singer, in her haunting song, "Is This All There Is?" shows us a classic rendition of this almost blues bound stage of recognition of the reality of the world we live in. But as we release our judgments seeing the world as it is changes. It becomes a place of clarity, a place where the world, one's life, and one's place in the reality of the universe can be looked at with a loving eye. In acceptance one is focused on one's own life, here one turns outward as well to see the world as it is for one's friends, for the culture's reoccurring dramas, for those caught in difficult circumstance, for those enmeshed in the often destructive drama of their lives; here feelings of compassion, one of the most sublime emotions, arises. Now, as the fruits of meditation occur in our everyday life, we have a point of reference that is the world at its natural luminescence. Through meditation we return again and again to this place of renewal that is the center of existence.

The next phase in the meditative process usually needs to be accepted from one who has some capacity as a meditator. The significance is that one needs to meditate inside a discipline that has the ability to begin reforming one's mind towards a more integrated condition. The meditation may need to be inside of something like mantra, visual exercises, or meditation on higher emotional function. If this is carried out on a significant enough level and towards a worthy end then the next phase can be extraordinary. This next level opens up the mind to manifest higher powers and greater emotional virtue and again requires the taking on of a fine discipline.

Running parallel to this and to a large extent both the precursor to the subtler energies of spirit and the result of reaching these subtler energies is the condition called mindfulness. This self-observation and action without judgment, now on the level of seeing—experiencing the world as it is—without the overlaying distortions of our own traumatic past or mental attempts to explain, justify, or protect ourselves, becomes the basis for an unencumbered movement through life. This is the basis for a freedom to truly act. Here the mind, the body, the emotions, the spirit are able to entertain an experience of the world as it is where we can act in concert with the reality of the universe that is us. Our experience and our meditation are the same and we find this new state to be one of extraordinary beauty and of the nature of poetry.

Finding the poem, one step from silence, can at this point be revealing. Michael McClure at the Beat Conference in New York in 1994 spoke of meditation and poetry. I paraphrase him here and surely mix my recollection with my own understanding. He spoke of the goals of meditation being our connection with universal reality and not the creating of poetry. But he spoke of the host of impressions that impinge on us daily; visual, auditory, dream images, emotional meetings with people familiar and unfamiliar, ideas that come to us through reading or conversation and how out of these millions of impressions only a small number leave their mark on us. As we sit in meditation at the close of the day some few of these many impressions stay with us, they form the content of our thought, they are the residue of our feeling and are the basis of our emotional life. In meditation we seek to release them and return our inner life to a calm reflection of universal reality. And yet, he said, these particular impressions, out of the many that invade us, have remained and we might seek in them the messages that they have for us. By gently nurturing them in poetry we might learn the lesson that they impart to us and through the refining process of turning them into art we might add to the glowing beauty of the world and pass along to others the fruit of our knowing.

The Meditation

The First Hour
Preparation

Preparation is important. Find a quiet place where you will be undisturbed for this First Hour of meditation. Create an alter that you can sit in front of. The alter is a place set aside in our busy life where silence and connection is the norm; it is a sacred place. On the alter place a candle, the flame a symbol of ourselves in the vastness of the universe; sandalwood incense, long used in scared ceremony to bring us deeply into a remembrance of our essential self; and a small vase with flowers, a representative of the beings of the natural world. Wear loose fitting clothing so that you are not constricted, especially around your waist. Reduce the lighting in the room and, sitting on a meditation pillow with crossed legs, find a comfortable position. Spend a few minutes just sitting.

Adjust your posture sitting with your torso straight, chin slightly tucked in. Feel as if a string were attached to the top of your head tugging gently as your spine aligns and your muscles loosen and relax.

Light the candle and the incense.

Meditation is a sacred undertaking where we seek a harmony between our interior life and the universal reality of which we are. To facilitate this undertaking we start and end each session with an act of self-recognition in the form of a posture with palms together over the heart, fingers tips at chin height, with torso slightly bent forward intoning OM, the Sanskrit syllable that includes all the sound of the universe.

Start with a Relaxation Exercise moving through your entire body until you feel a relaxing of muscles throughout, particularly around the neck and shoulders. Spend about ten minutes on this.

Now begin focusing on your breathing, letting your breath come from your belly; filling your lungs from bottom to top and breathing out from top to bottom using your diaphragm. Do this until you have a regular, rhythmic breathing pattern established. You are now ready to begin the first phase of Meditation.

Self-Observation

Self-Observation is the seemingly simple act of watching, as an observer, the content of one's thoughts; the effect of one's emotions; the nature of one's feelings; one's responses to stimuli; and the constant chatter that goes on in most people all the time. From self-criticism to feelings of abandonment; from a host of desires both good and not so good to the effects of past trauma; from the effects of success and moments of exhilaration to the longing for love and romance, one is engulfed in the story of one's past.

Sit for 20 minutes and observe the content of your thoughts. If you find yourself following one scenario or another, once you recognize that you are inside of the drama of it, return to Self-Observation.

Acceptance

Acceptance is one of the greatest and most difficult lessons of life. Whether life has been good or difficult; whether one is happy or sad; whether one feels unworthy of the good or unjustly oppressed by the bad the moment of acceptance is liberating. Acceptance is not resignation and it is not justification for intolerable acts committed either by oneself or by one person against another. It is the first moment of realization that this too is part of the universal reality and we are already in it and have always been part of it. The dramas of our life are and have always been but a part of the greater whole that is life. We have never been outside of it even when the good or the ill have been overwhelming. Acceptance is like a great sighing release of a fear that had no foundation; the revelation of a great trick played on oneself by oneself.

Sit for 20 minutes and observe the content of your thoughts and the impact of your emotions. Recognize that they are your life and that they will always be your life. As the many experiences of your life come to mind and to your memory, flooding your emotions, recognize them as your life and accept them as your life and that they will always be your life. Through this act of acceptance you begin to open yourself to the reality of life.

This concludes the first hour of meditation. Do an act of self-recognition and lay on your back for a few minutes and rest. Get up and take a walk.

Second Hour

The Second Hour should be done no sooner than four hours after the First Hour, it can be done the next day. Go through the same Preparation as before. You are now ready to go through the second phase of Meditation.

Light the incense and candle and do an act of self-recognition.

Continue as in the First Hour the act of Self-observation and Acceptance. For 20 minutes watch the content of your thoughts and the impact of your emotions and silently accept them as your life. As you go deeper into this phase you may encounter material that is more difficult to handle or content that is embarrassing or confusing or content that is very pleasant, you are now ready for the next step in meditation.

Letting-Go

Letting-Go is a most important and revealing process. In the first act of self-observation we found that to begin the process of gaining some facility with our mental and emotional life we had to continuously come back to self-observation whenever we found ourselves chasing the rabbit. In that simple act we began the process of Letting-Go. We let go of the relentless pursuit of our own thoughts.

We now apply that act more generally to all of the content we find that makes up our rather extraordinary inner life. As we come across past negative experiences floating in our memory we let them go. As we find places of tension in our body, we let them go. As we find snippets of ideas we let them go. As we find trauma from our past; abuses, betrayals, fears, hopelessness, we let the emotion rise in us and let go, let the tears come, let the sobs come through us, let the angry shout go, let our face distort in sadness, let the constriction of our heart release, letting-go of the past that so confines us and keeps us focused in a time that has past. And also, when moments of fun arise, when times of pleasure well up, let them go as well, they too keep us in the past. Both the pain and the pleasure are ours, they are the content of our life, they will always and forever be the stuff of our soulfulness but we let them go to find their rightful place in our past releasing the hold they have on our present and future. We do this with gentleness and fondness and sadness for with this Letting-Go we change our interior and something altogether new becomes possible. This is not to say that at some future time when we have learned more of our interior life we may not come back to both the good and the ill, but now we let them go

Sit for 20 minutes and recognize the content of your inner life letting-go of all that you find. Let go by silently saying "I Let go" or physically letting go of tensions or through your breath breathe out the content on an exhale and settle into regular deep breathing again. Let go in any manner you can but begin the process of letting-go of your past.

See The World As It Is

This next part of meditation may not come easily for some time but it can be started at this stage. Seeing The World As It Is is a natural step in the progression from self-observation to acceptance to letting-go. We now have the means of seeing the world with the filters of our mostly traumatic past off. It can be both exhilarating and quite sad, filled with grief for the life that one has lived and for what seems the inevitability of it. Seeing The World As It Is is both an act of forgiveness and an act of clarity. It is forgiveness of ourselves for the foolishness of so many of our acts. Here we recognize that we have lived our life without consciousness and it has often caused us and others pain and sadness. Clarity arises as we begin to see the nature of the continuing drama of our life; as we begin to see with filters removed. Though we may not now, or in fact ever, completely alter the drama of our life, we can see the drama of our life and, of all life around us, and in that recognition we can begin to act more in concert with the reality of the universe. We can begin the process of acting in concert with nature and with our place in it. We do this first by Seeing The World As It Is.

For 20 minutes sit quietly inside this place of recognizing The World As It Is. It is a place without judgment, and at this stage a place without action. It requires some time to find so be gentle on yourself.

This concludes the beginning stage of Meditation. This approach can be done over and over until one comes to it with a capacity to enter into meditation whenever and wherever it is needed. It becomes a glowing part of one's present life and is the means and the preparation both for allowing the past its rightful place in the past and preparing an opening for the future to enter unencumbered.

It is important to know that meditation of this sort does not preclude action. This is not intended as a means to succomb to a life of in-action. Rather it is the action of non-action where we act in-concert with nature, the universe, and are living a less encumbered life, one that is rich and creative. We will still falter but, we may have a way to redress our errors that is more gentle on us and on others.

A thousand years

to Laurene

I can't find you but I want to find you
Like a thousand years ago when we met
On a high mountain meadow the sun was low
And we again did not know where we were
We do not know now and are in a whole
Battery of tears we do not know from
Whence they came and yet here they are
Running like that damp rain pouring on us
It was before you were born when I was wandering
And wandering still you were coming and no one knew
Certainly me but then you were there and it was alright
Now you are again gone unborn again and I want to find you

Boy of Art Girl of Poetry

The day is long in the barrel of the green world
Standing as it is in the corner of this place
Hidden from the carnage going on below

Like drawing back to the place of beginning
When the earth shot out pillars of beauty
Large planes of love and truth rode bareback

Art was a boy young and beautiful   Poetry was a girl
Full of desire and they ran screaming
Into the arms of each other without knowing
The order of things

Flashing about in the grass of a dizzy afternoon sun

Caught not as a thief but caught in the shadow
Steps of a thief behind the satisfied gaze
Of the neighborhood

Never caught by any but the thief

The clear forehead of innocence that would make
The body whole   the hard muscular night
That would purge the soul of aliens

The wandering look that would start small magical
Inhabitants squelling with delight
Because it was coming.

That rift   the tear in the membrane   the veil that
Was pulled over the eyes
And the heart by snarling old man beast

It was falling and nothing could stop it
Not the jealous rage of age or the wire wrapping
Of fear could stop it and the inhabitants of the old
World prepared to bathe and reignite

As the boy of art and the girl of poetry entered each other
The curtain fell about them golden Smelling of soft music
Small points of light danced up out of the abyss
To which they had been exiled

And the boy of art and the girl of poetry
Became their people and without form
Were scattered over the earth into the
Rock faces and tree spirits and into small bodies
Of animals   into the neighborhoods
Where old ladies cried themselves to sleep
Where old men wondered at their cruel deeds so long go

And the golden cord went out   wrapped itself
Around the mad girl on the ward

It went out to the children   without fathers

It went out without stopping

The boy of art and the girl of poetry could not
Stop the love that boiled between them

Though finally the world came between

Even so   late at night when the air is quiet
And the dog barks lowly in the distance   long
Tendrils leave their solar plexus
And travel the many dark miles   to join
Them together in some hidden place
Among the small inhabitants of hillsides
And stream banks

And the tear is small   and the entrance reticent
But it goes on and it does not stop

And it goes on and on   and it is what love requires

Author Biography

John (poet) Peterson has been both an explorer in the intellectual sense and in the worldly sense. After traveling the country with his brother Craig, John spent many years in academia in a number of institutions following art and philosophy, doing graduate work in psychology, psycho-physiology and research into biofeedback. With two years in the military and the "war of our time" (Vietnam) there followed the concomitant political activism that was as inevitable as the confusion of a country. Doing post-graduate work in the emerging fields of holistic healing and consciousness development and then deeply engaging in poetry—finding a vehicle to make a deep statement about all of this—the result was a real sense of the possibilities that now exist.

The role of the intellect is to gain knowledge and then to take that knowledge out into the world. The foundation for an exploration into the society and the environments of nature, work, and culture took John into social services in the high mountains and then 25 years in management to, as it were, test the hypothesis of the preceding years, and raise a family. The test is as we see, a country still torn but with a grounding in a new and greater sense of its possibilities. The test also was of a personal sort and leaves some questions still to answer; the methods are there, the task is in the implementation, the nerve to do it.

John has published five books of poetry, and as publisher of Poetic Matrix Press over eighty books from a varied group of authors including poets Francisco X. Alarcon, Lyn Lifshin, Brandon Cesmat, James Downs, Gail Entrekin, Leroy Moore, Joe Milosch, Rayn Roberts and Sandra Stillwell. In a fine-dining career over 25 years John managed the Rueben E. Lee, a moored river boat on San Diego Bay, Princess Resort's Dockside on Mission Bay, Kung Food Vegetarian Restaurant, one of the premier vegetarian restaurants in the country, and two rooms in Yosemite; at the 150 year old Wawona Hotel and the magnificent Mountain Room at Yosemite Lodge at the Falls with one of the most beautiful views in the world, viewing Yosemite Falls through three stories of windows. The test in all instances was to implement the tenets of the poetic matrix for all involved. John is retired from management and devotes full time to writing and publishing.

Appendix

Appendix

Exercises

Chart

Relaxation Time

Find yourself a quiet, secluded location where you won't be disturbed for the next 20 minutes. Remove your shoes, loosen your belt or tight clothing. Find a comfortable chair or lie on the floor. Put on some soft, low music, place a vase of flowers on a table near you and light some pleasant incense. This is a time to relax.

Stretch out, arms resting by your side, feet slightly apart, eyes gently closed.

Think to yourself, "I am going to relax completely, at the end I will feel fully refreshed."

Feel your feet, wiggle your toes, flex your ankles. Then "let go" - let go of all the tension, and let your feet rest limp and heavy.

Feel the lower part of your legs, your knees, and thighs, up to your hips. Imagine them just sinking into the floor, heavy and relaxed.

Now feel your hands. Wiggle your fingers and flex your wrists, then "let go", relax.

Feel your lower arms, elbows and upper arms, up to your shoulders, let them drop.

Picture all the tension just melting away.

Feel your abdomen. Let the tension go, allow your breath to flow into your abdomen.

Feel your chest, up to your throat and neck. As you continue breathing more deeply into your belly, imagine all the tension flowing out, relax more and more.

Feel your face, and across your scalp. Release the tension in your jaw, open your mouth slightly, and part you teeth and lips. Feel relaxation flow across your face.

Check your entire body and where you feel tension release it letting your entire body relax deeply and fully.

Remain in this completely relaxed state for five to ten minutes. If you dose off for a few minutes that's OK, the relaxation is deepening.

When you are ready to be active again say to yourself, "I have been deeply relaxed, I am now ready to continue my day fully refreshed."

Begin to move by flexing your ankles, wiggle your toes, wiggle your fingers and shake your wrists. Bend your legs and stretch your arms. Open your eyes, you are ready to continue your day, but first sit for a time and recognize the condition you have achieved. Feel and remember the well-being throughout your body.

Adapted from Barbara Brown's *Stress and Biofeedback*

Moving the Body

Stand amongst the greenery of the earth.

With feet shoulder width apart and knees slightly bent hold an imaginary ball dark red in color and one foot in diameter in front of your belly. Close your eyes.

Begin a gentle turning motion from your hips keeping your shoulders and head in alignment. Turn from side to side.

As you move let the ball increase in size to three feet and then back to one foot, decrease its size to four inches and then back. Let your hands flow across the ball first on top and then underneath as you turn from side to side.

Relax your shoulders and continue turning from side to side.

Tense all the muscles of your body as you continue in a flowing motion turning from side to side with the dark red ball held out in front breathing fully as you turn from deep within your hips.

Relax once again and slow your movement down as you continue to turn. Let the motions come in a free and flowing manner. Continue for ten minutes alternating tensing and releasing, increasing and decreasing the size of the ball, continuously turning from side to side. Let the movement come smoothly and with ease.

Stop the movement and stand with eyes closed and experience your body and the sensation of your physiology.

Breath deep and give thanks for the beauty of your body.

Breathing into the Body

Breathing into the Body is the first experience that integrates the inner and outer aspects of ourselves. Breathing represents the mid-point between the psychological and the physiological and forms a link between the energy in our body and that of the natural world around us. Breathing into the Body brings about a state of deep relaxation and integration to mind and body. It is the first physiological activity that goes on all the time without conscious intervention that we can join with consciously and have an effect on.

The lungs are divided into three parts: the upper part, the middle part, and the lower part. Normally we breathe only with the upper portion of the lungs. First, inhale, filling the lungs from the top down to the bottom; do this for one minute. This is our usual manner of breathing.

Breathing into the Body:

Sit in a comfortable manner in a chair or on the floor with a meditation pillow under you.

Your spine straight and relaxed.

Your belly relaxed, belts loosened.

Your chin tucked in.

Your shoulders low and relaxed.

Your hands in your lap, back of your right hand in the palm of the your left hand.

Inhale filling the lower part of your lungs first, then the middle, then the upper.

Exhale in the reverse order.

Continue for two minutes.

The diaphragm is a dome-shaped muscle attached to the bottom of the rib cage. When we inhale it contracts, flattening down and out, pulling air into the lungs. When we exhale it relaxes, rising and pushing the air out of the lungs. Inhale as above from the bottom to the middle to the top of the lungs and this time let your belly push out drawing the diaphragm down and pulling the air into your lungs.

Continue this Breathing into the Body for 5 minutes. Do this breathing whenever you get the opportunity until it becomes the normal breathing pattern; especially in stressful situations.

Adapted from The Arica Institute exercise Dia-Kath Breathing

The Alpha Nap

A meditative session as short as 20 minutes can have a positive effect on well-being. The following exercise is a short, 20 minute maximum, simple process of enhancing alpha, leading to a rapid recovery from a tired, exhausted condition. It is particularly useful immediately after a work session when one wishes to be alert and refreshed.

Find a comfortable place on a couch or soft recliner. It should be a place associated with an easy-going rather than a formal circumstance.

Sit in a posture that is casual, head propped against your hand or lean back on the head rest. It is a posture that would only be comfortable for a short time.

Take a deep breath, close your eyes, and then let your mind wander, focusing on nothing in particular.

If you find yourself thinking about something let go of it and again let your mind wander. Continue to take deep breathes.

Let your body sink deeper into the material of the couch or chair.

Continue in this way, after a period of time you will become aware of lucid mental material but only momentarily.

You will then find yourself awakening after having dozed for a very short time.

You will feel refreshed and very lucid, ready to continue your activity.

This is the Alpha Nap!!!

Chart of Feedback and Feedforward

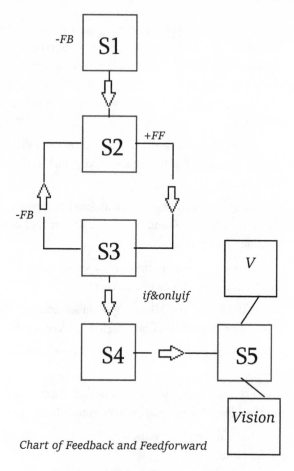

Chart of Feedback and Feedforward

-FB	Negative Feedback
+FF	Positive Feedforward
S1	Gaining Control
S2	Unresponsive/Low Arousal/Relaxed State
S3	Recognizing the Goal
if&onlyif	If and Only If
S4	Process of Altering the Signal
S5	New State Realized
V	Process Complete without Introspection
Vision	Process Complete with Introspection

Endnotes

The Healing Body Part I

1. Elizabeth Reninger, *"Wu Wei: the Action of Non-Action,"* http://taoism.about.com/od/wuwei/a/wuwei.htm.

2. *"Definition of feedback,"* Merriam-Webster; http://www.merriam-webster.com/dictionary/feedback.

3. Wikibooks; https://en.wikibooks.org/wiki/Control_Systems/Feedback_Loops Negative vs Positive Feedback12.

4. *Principles of Holistic Healing Support our Whole Self,* http://www.edgemagazine.net/2010/10/principles-of-holistic-healing/.

5. Linda Ann S.H. Tom, M.D., *Health and Health Care for CHINESE-AMERICAN ELDERS,* http://web.stanford.edu/group/ethnoger/chinese.html.

6. Ralph Waldo Emerson, *"Over-soul,"* from Essays: First Series, 1841.

7. Charles Tart, ed., *Altered States of Consciousness,* (New York: Anchor Books, 1969).

8. Larry Rouse, John Peterson, and Gary Shairo, *"EEG alpha entrainment reaction within the biofeedback setting and some possible effects on epilepsy,"* Physiological Psychology 1975, Vol. 3.

9. Joneis Thomas, *"Biofeedback."* Gale Encyclopedia of Mental Disorders. 2003. Encyclopedia.com. 13 Feb. 2011 <http://www.encyclopedia.com>.

10. *"The core body temperature homeostat;"* https://en.wikipedia.org/wiki/Homeostasiso.

12. Wikioedia; https://en.wikipedia.org/wiki/Nociceptor.

12. Wikipedia; https://en.wikipedia.org/wiki/Antoni_Gaudi.

13. Thich Nhat Hanh; *The Diamond That Cuts Through Illusion,* (Berkeley: Parallax Press, 1992).

14. Wilhelm Reich, *The Mass Psychology of Fascism,* (New York: Farrar, Straus & Giroux,1970).

15. Thomas Kuhn, *The Structure of Scientific Revolutions,* (Chicago: The University of Chicago Press), 1962, 12.

16. Marilyn Ferguson, *Aquarian Conspiracy,* (New York: Penguin, 1980).

17. Elmer Green and Alice Green, *Beyond Biofeedback*, (New York: Random House, 1977).

18. Aldous Huxley, *The Doors of Perception*, (New York: Harper Collins, 1954).

19. Garth Kemerling, *Philosophy Pages* (philosophypages.com).

20, 21, 22, 23, 24, 25, 26, Ideologies, various as found on Wikipedia.com.

27. Mircea Eliade, *The Sacred And The Profane*, (New York: Harcourt Brace Jovanovich, 1957).

28. Eliade, *The Sacred And The Profane*.

Healing the Planet Part II

1. C.A. Meier, *Wilderness and the Search for the Soul of Modern Man.*
2. From the forward by Robert Hinshaw to *A Testament to the Wilderness, Ten Essays on an address by C.A. Meier.*
3. Jessie Weston, *Ritual to Romance* (1920),
4. Wolfram von Eschenbach, *Parzival,* (New York: Vintage Books 1961).
5. Sarah Frances Vanneste, *The Black Death And The Future Of Medicine,* https://digitalcommons.wayne.edu/oa_theses/29.
6. Terence Mckenna, *Food of the Gods,* (New York: Bantam New Age Books, 1993).
7. Michael Crichton, Jurissic Park.
8.Aldo Leopold, *A Sand County Almanac,* (New York: Oxford University Press, 1949).
9. *Introduction to Salmon: Running the Gauntlet,* May 1, 2011 on PBS, Nature.
10. Terence Mckenna, *Food of the Gods*
11. Novalis, *Friedrich Leopold, Freiherr von (baron of) Hardenberg, (born May 2, 1772, Oberwiederstedt, Prussian Saxony [Germany]— died March 25, 1801, Weissenfels, Saxony [Germany]), early German Romantic poet and theorist who greatly influenced later Romantic thought.*

Poetry, Poets, the Poem and the Political Process Part III

1. McCarthy Film.com - *Selected Poems* by Eugene J. McCarthy, ...
https://www.mccarthyfilm.com/gene-selected-poems
2. Jimmy Carter, *Always a Reckoning*, 1995 (from the website www.bong-town.com/Bong_Town/Liberia/Poems/firestone.html
3. Wilfred Owens, *The Parable of the Old Man and the Young*
4. Poems of Mao Zedong - Marxists Internet Archive
https://www.marxists.org/reference/archive/mao/.
5. Ho Chi Minh, *Poems Written While In Prison* | Poem
https://motherbird.com/hochi.html
6. Walt Whitman, preface to *Leaves of Grass* (1855)

A Discussion of Poetics: the Development of Wholistic Forms of Consciousness and Poetry Part IV

1. Fyodor Dostoevsky, *The Dream of a Ridiculous Man,* 1877.

2. Charles Baudelair, From *Fuses 1 - on God,* Translated from the French by Norman Cameron

3. *Art of El Greco,* https://en.wikipedia.org/wiki/Art_of_El_Greco

4. Pablo Picasso, *Picasso speaking of Les Demoiselles d'Avignon to Dor de la Souchère in Antibes.*

5. Barry Miles, *Ginsburg A Biography,* (New York: Perennial. 1989).

6. Miles, *Ginsburg A Biography.*

7. Oscar Ichazo, Oscar, *Between Metaphysics and Protoanalysis,* (New York: Arica Institute Press, 1984).

8. Ichazo, *Between Metaphysics and Protoanalysis.*

9. John White, ed., *The Highest State of Cousciousness,* (New York: Anchor Books, 1972).

10. Jack Kerouac, *The Scripture of the Golden Eternity,* (San Francisco: City Lights Books: 1994).

11. Alan Watts, *The Modern Mystic,* (Great Britain: Element Books 1990).

12. Ichazo, *Between Metaphysics and Protoanalysis.*

13. Ann Charters, *The Portable Beat Reader,* (New York: Penguin Books, 1992).

14. Charters, *The Portable Beat Reader*

15. Gia-Fu Feng, trans., *Tao te Ching,* (New York: Vintage Books, 1972).

16. Tomislav Budak, *TRIALECTICS -LOGIC FOR A NEW MILLENNIUM,* Formal, Dialectical and Trialectical Axioms from his 1995 essay.

17. Justin Kaplan, *Walt Whitman A Life,* (New York: BantamBooks: 1982).

18. Arthur Elsen, *The Book of Musical Knowledge,* (New York: Houghton Mifflin Company, 1927).

19. Gustave Reese, *In the Middle Ages,* (New York: W.W. Norton & Company, 1940).

20. Snyder, Gary, *The Real Work,* (New York: New Directions Books, 1980).

21. David Meltzer, ed., *The San Francisco Poets,* (New York: Ballantine Books, 1971).

22. Octavio Paz, *Convergences: Essays on Art and Literature*, (San Diego: Harcourt Brace Jovanovich, 1987).

23. Meltzer, ed., *The San Francisco Poets*.

24. Alfred Einstein, *Essay on Music*, (New York: W.W. Norton Co., 1956).

25. Einstein, *Essay on Music*.

26. Einstein, *Essay on Music*.

27. J.W.N. Sullivan, *Beethoven*, (New York: Mentor Books, 1927).

28. Meltzer, ed., *The San Francisco Poets*.

29. Einstein, *Essay on Music*.

30. Snyder, *The Real Work*.

31. Kaplan, *Walt Whitman A Life*.

32. Ichazo, *Between Metaphysics and Protoanalysis*.

33. Ursula Vaughan Williams, *Silence and Music*, (New Jersey: Essential Books, 1959).

34. Louise Bogan *A Poet's Alphabet*, (New York: McGraw Hill Books Company, 1979).

35. Bogan, *A Poet's Alphabet*.

36. Kaplan, *Walt Whitman A Life*.

37. James Karman, *Robinson Jeffers Poet of California*, (San Francisco: Chronicle Books, 1987).

38. Robert Bly, ed., *News of the Universe*, (San Francisco: Sierra Club Books, 1980).

39. Karman, *Robinson Jeffers Poet of California*.

40. Robinson Jeffers, *Selected Poems*, (New York: Vintage Books, 1965).

41. Jeffers, *Selected Poems*.

42. Meltzer, ed., *The San Francisco Poets*.

43. Charters, *The Portable Beat Reader*.

44. Meltzer, ed., *The San Francisco Poets*.

45. Meltzer, ed., *The San Francisco Poets*.

46. Pablo Neruda, *Canto General*, (Berkeley: University California Press, 1991).

47. Neruda, *Canto General*.

48. Neruda, *Canto General*.

49. Snyder, *The Real Work*.

50. Feng, trans., *Tao te Ching*.

51. Feng, trans., *Tao te Ching*.

52. Meltzer, ed., *The San Francisco Poets*

53. Robert E. Horn, ed., *Trialectics, Toward a Practical Logic of Unity,* *(Lexington, Mass:* Lexington Institute Publications, 1983).

54. Rainer Maria Rilke,*Sonnets To Orpheus,* (New York: W.W. Norton & Company, 1942).

55. Rilke, *Sonnets To Orpheus.*

56. Ichazo, *Between Metaphysics and Protoanalysis.*

57. Ichazo, *Between Metaphysics and Protoanalysis.*

58. Shinkichi Takahashi, *Afterimages: Zen Poems,* (New York: Anchor Books, 1972).

59. Charters, *The Portable Beat Reader.*

60. Meltzer, ed., *The San Francisco Poets*

61. Snyder, *The Real Work.*

62. M. C. Richards, *Centering In Pottery, Poetry, and the Person,* Middletown Connecticut: Wesleyan University Press, 1962).

63. Meltzer, ed., *The San Francisco Poets.*

64. Thomas Merton, *The Way of Chuang Tzu,(New York:* New Directions, 1965).

65. Gary Snyder, *Axe Handles,* (San Francisco: North Point Press, 1983).

Selected Bibliography

Bly, Robert, ed. *News of the Universe.* San Francisco: Sierra Club.

Eliade, Mircea. *The Sacred And The Profane.* New York: Harcourt Brace Jovanovich, 1a957.

Einstein, Alfred. *Essay on Music.* New York: W.W. Norton Co., 1956.

Fergeson, Marilyn. *The Aquarian Conspiracy.* Jeremy P. Tarcher/ Penguin, 1980.

Green, Elmer, and Alyce Green. Beyond Biofeedback. Delacorte Press, 1977.

Hanh, Thich Nhat. *The Diamond That Cuts Through Illusion.* Parallax Press, 2010.

Horn, Robert E. ed. *Trialectics, Toward a Practical Logic of Unity,*

Huxley, Aldous. *The Doors of Percetion & Heaven and Hell.* Harper & Brothers, 1954.

Ichazo, Oscar. *Between Metaphysics and Protoanalysis.* New York: Arica Institute Press, 1984.

Kaplan, Justin. *Walt Whitman A Life.* New York: BantamBooks: 1982.

Kuhn, Thomas. *The Structure of Scientific Revolutions.* Chicago: The University of Chicago Press, 1962.

Lexington, Mass: Lexington Institute Publications, 1983.

Leopold, Aldo. *A Sand County Almanac.* New York: Oxford University Press, 1949.

Lilly, John C. *Programming and Metaprogramming in the Human Biocomputer: Theory and Experiments.* Three Rivers Press, 1972.

Lorca, Federico Garcia. *The Duende: Theory and Divertissement.* The Poet's Work. Reginald Gibbons ed.

Mckenna, Terence. *Food of the Gods.* New York: Bantam New Age Books, 1993.

Meltzer, David ed. *The San Francisco Poets. New York:* Ballantine Books, 1971.

Merton, Thomas. *The Way of Chuang Tzu. New York:* New Directions, 1965.

Miles, Barry. *Ginsburg A Biography.* New York: Perennial. 1989.

Naranho, Claudio. *The One Quest.* The Viking Press, 1972.

Neruda, Pablo. *Canto General.* Berkeley: University California Press, 1991.

Reich, Wilhelm. *The Mass Psychology of Fascism.* New York: Farrar, Straus & Giroux, 1970.

Rilke, Rainer Maria. *Sonnets To Orpheus,* New York: W.W. Norton & Company, 1942.

Richards, M.C.. *Centering In Pottery, Poetry, and the Person,* Wesleyan University Press: Middletown Connecticut, 1962.

Snyder, Gary. *Axe Handles,* San Francisco: North Point Press, 1983.

Tart, Charles T. ed. Altered States of Consciousness. Doubleday Anchor Books, 1972.

Watts, Alan. *The Modern Mystic.* Great Britain: Element Books 1990.

Whitman, Walt. *Leaves of Grass.* 1855.

White, John ed. *The Highest State of Cousciousness.* Anchor Books, 1972.

Publications

Papers

Larry Rouse, John Peterson, and Gary Shairo, *EEG alpha entrainment reaction within the biofeedback setting and some possible effects on epilepsy,* Physiological Psychology 1975, Vol. 3.
John Peterson, *A Place In Which We Can Live,* The No-Street Poet's Voice, September 1987.
John Peterson, *Why do this?,* Poetic Matrix Newsletter, 1997.
John Peterson and Jack Seileman, *Wisdom of the Natural World,* New Vision Journal, October 1992.
John Peterson, *Wilderness in the City,* Canary, February/March 2009.
John Peterson, *I Am a White Male,* SISYPHUS, 2017.
John (poet) C Peterson *How Can Progressives Protect the "Atmosphere" of a Democratic Presidency,* Academia.edu, 2020.
John (poet) C Peterson, *I Am a White Male,* Academia.edu, 2020
John (poet) Peterson, *Wilderness in the City,* Academia.edu, 2021.

Books

John Peterson and Thomas Gayton, *Two Races One Face Two Faces One Race,* DruryLane Press, 1994.
John, *Poetry of Dark Hills and Wild Mountains,* Poetic Matrix Press, 2001.
John, *News of the Day poems of the times,* Poetic Matrix Press, 2007.
John, *The Nature of Mountains,* Kvasir Books, 2017.
John Peterson, James Downs & Joe Milosch, Editors, *So Many Voices Authors' 20th Anniversary Anthology 1997 to 2017,* Cover Art by Molly Weller, Poetic Matrix Press, 2017.
John, *Amtrak Starbucks Jazz on the Streets of Richmond,* Kvasir Books, 2018.

Publisher, Poetic Matrix Press, 1997-2021.